DOCTOR
ON EVEREST

DOCTOR ON EVEREST

PETER STEELE

RAINCOAST BOOKS

Vancouver

Raincoast Books acknowledges the ongoing financial support of the Government of Canada through The Canada Council for the Arts and the Book Publishing Industry Development Program (BPIDP); and the Government of British Columbia through the BC Arts Council.

Edited by Scott Steedman
Text design and typesetting by Teresa Bubela
Line drawings by Phoebe Bullock
Photographs by the author unless noted otherwise

LIBRARY AND ARCHIVES CANADA CATALOGUING IN PUBLICATION

Steele, Peter, 1935-
    Doctor on Everest : a memoir of the ill-fated 1971
international Everest expedition/ Peter Steele.

Includes index.
ISBN 1-55192-765-9

    1. Steele, Peter, 1935-. 2. International Himalayan Expedition, 1971.
3. Mountaineering expeditions--Everest, Mount (China and Nepal) I. Title.

GV199.92.S73A3 2005   796.5'222'092
C2005-900340-5

LIBRARY OF CONGRESS CATALOGUE NUMBER: [insert LOC]

Raincoast Books   In the United States:
9050 Shaughnessy Street   Publishers Group West
Vancouver, British Columbia   1700 Fourth Street
Canada V6P 6E5   Berkeley, California
www.raincoast.com   94710

At Raincoast Books we are committed to protecting the environment and to the responsible use of natural resources. We are acting on this commitment by working with suppliers and printers to phase out our use of paper produced from ancient forests. This book is one step towards that goal. It is printed on 100% ancient-forest-free paper (100% post-consumer recycled), processed chlorine- and acid-free, and supplied by New Leaf paper. It is printed with vegetable-based inks. For further information, visit our website at www.raincoast.com. We are working with Markets Initiative (www.oldgrowthfree.com) on this project.

Printed in Canada by Friesens
10 9 8 7 6 5 4 3 2 1

To Adam, Judith and Lucy and theirs

In all it may be said that one factor beyond all others is required for success. Too many chances are against the climbers; too many contingencies may turn against them. Anything like a breakdown of the transport will be fatal; soft snow on the mountain will be an impregnable defence; a big wind will send back the strongest; even so small a matter as a boot fitting a shade too tight may endanger one man's foot and involve the whole party in retreat. The climbers must have above all things, if they are to win through, good fortune, and the greatest good fortune of all for mountaineers, some constant spirit of kindness in Mount Everest itself, the forgetfulness for long enough of its more cruel moods; for we must remember that the highest of mountains is capable of severity, a severity so awful and so fatal that the wiser sort of men do well to think and tremble even on the threshold of their high endeavour.

GEORGE LEIGH MALLORY (1886–1924)

INTERNATIONAL HIMALAYAN EXPEDITION 1971

Leaders
Norman Dyhrenfurth (Switzerland/U.S.A.)
James Roberts (U.K.)

Climbers

Wolfgang Axt (Austria)	Carlo Mauri (Italy)
Harka Bahadur Gurung (Nepal)	Pierre Mazeaud (France)
Harsh Bahuguna (India)	David Peterson (U.S.A.)
Duane Blume (U.S.A.)	Leo Schlömmer (Austria)
Gary Colliver (U.S.A.)	Peter Steele (U.K.)
Odd Eliassen (Norway)	Jon Teigland (Norway)
John Evans (U.S.A.)	Naomi Uemura (Japan)
Dougal Haston (U.K.)	Michel Vaucher (Switzerland)
Toni Hiebeler (W. Germany)	Yvette Vaucher (Switzerland)
David Isles (U.S.A.)	Don Whillans (U.K.)
Reizo Ito (Japan)	

BBC

John Cleare	Ian Stuart
Ian Howell	Juréc Surdel (Poland)
Ned Kelly	Antony Thomas
Bill Kurban	

Sunday Times
Murray Sayle

FOREWORD

THIS STORY takes place more than thirty years ago. Recently I re-read the book with a view to bringing certain parts of it up to date, according to what we now know about mountain sickness and some of the other medical details. However, I soon realized that altering the text would alter the flavour of a book that was written when the journey to Everest was less cluttered than it is today. So with all its imperfections, I offer to you a very personal account of what it was like to be a doctor on an expedition to the highest mountain in the world. It is no joyride, and I hope that the flavour of the unpleasant parts of an expedition and the courage and despair of the participants come through. Should you notice errors — whether they be medical or technical climbing ones — please view them in the light of the advance in knowledge accrued over the past three decades since all this happened. Despite all the problems we encountered, this expedition remains one of the highlights of my life, spent in close proximity to some of the finest people I have ever had the privilege to meet.

PETER STEELE, WHITEHORSE, YUKON, 2004

INTRODUCTION

"NOTHING IS MORE conducive to irritation than incivility, or uncontrolled passing of wind." Spoken like a true climber! Or, more accurately, a British climber. A youthful Doctor Peter Steele jotted that light-hearted observation in his diary a few meals into the seminal 1971 International Everest Expedition. As one of the two high-altitude doctors on the massive team, he had occasion to share his gracious bedside manners with some of the last century's greatest Himalayan climbers. And high-altitude flatulence was one of the lesser afflictions that visited the expedition.

I have come to know Peter Steele well in the past twenty-five years. In 1979 I shot my first of two picture books about the Yukon. One of the most dramatic photos in it showed a sailboat far out on Atlin Lake, the Llewelyn Glacier glistening in the Coast Range behind. I did not know Peter then, and did not know that he was the boat's skipper. We didn't actually meet till a couple of years later. It was January, the temperature hovering around minus thirty Celsius, when I knocked on his door in Whitehorse. In those days, his house was a crash pad for itinerant travelers, as it still is.

Three Czech climbers, fresh off a winter climb of a nearby peak named, coincidentally, Mount Steele (at 5,073m, Canada's fifth highest mountain), sprawled on his living-room floor, feet elevated on cushions. Their hands clutched half-empty beer bottles and big grins spread across their bearded faces. Their toes and parts of their feet were the colour of coal. Peter was fussing about, changing the dressing he had put on their frostbitten limbs a few hours before and quizzing them on how the climb had gone.

Looking back on that scene, it's easy for me to imagine how well suited he was for his duties on the '71 expedition. With some thirty

climbers and forty Sherpas, the expedition was one of the largest before
the pestilence of commercialization infected Everest in the early '90s, and
the medical needs were staggering. Luckily for everyone concerned,
Peter's experience on remote treks in Nepal, Bhutan and Canada's rugged
Labrador coast put him in good stead. Just a few years before, while
trekking solo in the shadow of Annapurna in western Nepal, he had come
across a dying Tibetan lama being read his last rites. Recognizing the
problem as a strangulated intestine, Peter reluctantly performed an emergency operation, while the holy man's entourage in the tent next door
summoned up the gods with horns and cymbals. His scalpel was a pocket
knife, the anaesthetic a shot of rakshi, the locally brewed spirit.

On Everest, Peter's knowledge of Nepali allowed him to eavesdrop
on the Sherpas' conversations in order to gauge what was really happening on the mountain. This broad knowledge of all things Himalayan
informs every aspect of this wonderful book. By his own admission, Peter
has never been drawn to large groups in the mountains. However, given
the seriousness of the 1971 undertaking, to attempt a sporting new route
on the steep 2,000-metre southwest face, he was willing to join forces
with these elite athletes.

Towards the end of the expedition, when sickness, poor food and
atrocious weather took its toll, the team was tempted to change course.
Peter writes that, rather than switch over to the far easier South Col route,
"we found it preferable to fail honourably on the route we had come
to climb than succeed on a route that had already seen 23 westerners."
Contrast that attitude with the prevalent one today, when legions of
affluent, under-qualified clients grope their way up a fixed rope that runs
all the way from the internet café tent at base camp to the summit on the
South Col route, which has now seen more than a thousand ascents.

The nearly successful '71 expedition laid the groundwork for the Brits
to come along in '75 and take the line of least resistance up the southwest
face. Not to be outdone, the Russians arrived a few years later and established "the line of most resistance," a highly technical rock route up the
southwest pillar, putting no fewer than eleven climbers on the summit.

This truly remarkable feat wouldn't have been possible without the lofty benchmarks established in 1971.

This story is as much an exposé of the colourful characters of Peter's famous climbing companions, foreign and Sherpa, as a chronology of the perilous day-to-day drudgery of attempting a difficult new route on the world's highest mountain. Anyone yearning for a good climbing tale, or seeking in-depth cultural advice about travel in the Himalayas, will find all this and more in the following pages.

PAT MORROW
CANMORE, ALBERTA, 2004

CHAPTER 1

M ount Everest Base Camp is a horrible place. Utter desolation. Immense boulders balance on slender frozen pedestals and dirty moraine rocks are scattered at random on a humpback of ice as though some giant in Tibet has hurled his garbage over the Lho La.

From the satanic steep enclosing walls of Lingtren, rocks thunder down narrow gullies. Ice cliffs break off from the hanging glaciers of Pumori and hurtle off the mountain face, gathering stones and snow and pushing ahead a white cloud of fine dust that spreads out across the debris cone. The roars are repeated throughout the night and we awake to the sound of an avalanche that peals off regularly about 6:30 a.m. and which we call "the milk train." The sun creeps over the Western Shoulder of Everest, its rays striking the Khumbu glacier. The rime of freezing night melts from the tent roof and the hoarfrost on beard and moustache softens. A Himalayan crow, the gorak, is up early to scavenge our last night's meal and the refuse of a dozen previous expeditions. Lammergeier vultures circle overhead slowly, watchfully, with sinister expectancy.

The Icefall is still in shadow. Before the sun picks out the relief of its contorted features it appears to be a peaceful staircase up to the Western Cwm of Everest, but the dawn reveals its icy chaos as a jumbled, frozen morass. This ever-moving river of ice spills over the sill of the Western Cwm like lava emptying from the rim of a volcanic crater and discharges its effluent onto the Khumbu glacier. It flows due south below the face of Nuptse, which forms a spire soaring skywards, its lower part plunging towards ice cliffs that hang suspended above the glacier.

From the grey mass of broken rock of the moraine, ribbed along its length, ice pinnacles rise in eerie fantastic shapes and caverns of ghostly blue ice are formed under high towers. This place is named Phantom Alley.

Clouds roll up the valley from the south and flurries turn to a snow-storm by afternoon and coldness descends on the camp, so we put our heavy down clothes back on again.

Night falls and so does the temperature. The blood is chilled; the air is thin, so breathing comes quick and short and irregular; my head aches with a dull throbbing and sleep will not come; home is a long way off and many dangers lie ahead.

THE MORNING FOLLOWING our arrival at Base Camp — March 24, 1971 — was one of feverish activity for the members of the expedition. We had assimilated our new surroundings and settled into the little orange tents that would be the strange substitute for home during the next two months. The moraine was so uneven that tents could only be pitched after the ground had been cleared of rocks and levelled with ice axes by the Sherpas. The appearance was unlike the regular lines of tents at our acclimatization camp on the flat-floored valley at Pheriche that had the military look of Younghusband's encampment on the plain before Lhasa.

A mood of cheerfulness and energy pervaded the camp despite the altitude, to which none of us was yet fully acclimatized, so we still became breathless from energetic work. I had suggested that the selection of a latrine area should be an early priority to ensure that our drinking water

did not become contaminated. Early in the morning I gathered some vol-
unteers and we set off across the stream beyond a pile of boulders a
hundred yards from camp with Jimmy Roberts' cry, "I'll go where I like,
and certainly not alongside all of you!" ringing in our ears. Odd Eliassen
from Norway, being a carpenter by trade, took charge of the building with
his friend Jon Teigland. He laid two wooden planks, brought up for
crevasses, side by side, with a gap between, over a pit built of stones. Lem
Putt would have been proud of the final construction.

Meanwhile the Japanese Naomi Uemura had decided he preferred a
view northwards to the Icefall and was arranging stones for footplaces
across a nearby narrow crevasse, and Reizo Ito, his compatriot, was crown-
ing this achievement with a cairn of stones. The two American Davids,
Peterson, doctor of medicine, and Isles, doctor of mathematics, were busy
behind a large boulder fifty yards upwind and summoned us to see their
creation. Tucked under the lee of an overhang, penned with a small wall,
was a triangular one-holer of elegant proportions dedicated solely to our
Swiss lady, Yvette Vaucher. Juréc Surdel applied his Polish artistic talent
to building a *pissoir*, labelled accordingly, at the entrance to the place but
sadly it was soon put to the wrong use by a non-French-speaking member.
Within an hour the area was transformed; it remained serviceable till the
end of the expedition and even Jimmy Roberts visited it twice a week.

The drinking water supply came from a frozen pool on the opposite
side of the camp, not many yards from the kitchen and kept sacrosanct —
until I found a member of the French Parliament cleaning his teeth in it.

"*Merde, ces médecins,*" Pierre Mazeaud expostulated with a shrug when
censured.

The Sherpas also set to work, showing even more skill in their construction, which was placed on the opposite side of camp to ours, sited
across a long, deep crevasse; observing hierarchy, the upper end was
reserved for sirdars, or leaders; the middle for high-altitude Sherpas; and
the bottom for Icefall porters and kitchen workers.

The kitchen and storeroom were placed a few yards from the hospital
in the middle of the camp. They were supervised by Danu, who had been

cook on many big expeditions, and any prima donna tendencies he showed were amply excused by the excellence of his yak stew and the elegance and lightness of his sponge cakes.

Danu was building his kingdom with dry stone walls. Arranged in boxes around the walls was a bizarre selection of the 20,900 pounds (9,500 kilograms) of food that had been shipped from Europe, comprising nearly three hundred porter-loads.

In the double mess tent the joint leaders of the expedition, Swiss-born Norman Dyhrenfurth and British ex-Gurkha colonel James Roberts, were conferring. Their monumental problem was to move thirty-odd tons of food and equipment and about fifty men up the Icefall into the Western Cwm of Mount Everest from where a two-pronged assault on the highest mountain in the world would begin. The two Sherpa sirdars, Sona Girme and Lhakpa Khumjung, were standing nearby to receive their orders. The gas lamps burned late into the night and numerous pieces of paper were covered in calculations and plans for the next few days.

Beside the mess tent John Evans, an American, was occupied in sharing the mountain of equipment boxes between the two teams — Face and West Ridge. Coils of red and blue nylon rope, ice hammers, pitons, crash helmets, air mattresses and other technical paraphernalia had to be apportioned equally and Wolfgang Axt from Austria, the other team coordinator, shared this job. His countryman, Leo Schlömmer, a mountain rescue expert, was attending to the wire winches that were intended for hauling or lowering loads on the Face of the mountain.

In a makeshift workshop outside his tent, Michel Vaucher, Yvette's husband, completed the job that he had started in Kathmandu, of fixing crampons onto the high-altitude boots. Because we had come from all over the world, we had had no previous chance to be fitted for our equipment, which had been gauged from measurements we supplied by mail. Toni Hiebeler, our West German climber, who had designed the heavy double-skinned boots to protect us from the ravages of frostbite, was making sure that they fitted properly.

Beside their tent the British pair, Don Whillans and Dougal Haston, were sharpening their crampon points with a metal file and checking over the climbing harnesses, on which their safety would depend when they were suspended on the Face in the weeks ahead.

In the food store, built close beside the kitchen, Gary Colliver (U.S.A.) took over the thankless job of making up the high-altitude rations, which are usually boxed before an expedition sets off. Carlo Mauri, from Italy, helped make up the food packs to last two men for two days high on the mountain; for example, he took a packet of nuts from one box, a tin of sardines from another and made an assortment of foods in blue plastic sacks.

A pile of planks and logs, looking strangely out of place in these tree-less surroundings, was being sorted by Harsh Bahuguna, an Indian Army climber. These were to be used for bridging the crevasses that cut deep into the substance of the glacier, barring our progress up the Icefall. Set at a safe distance from camp, the green oxygen cylinders were stored, racked like artillery shells in preparation to bombard the mountain. Duane Blume, an American physiologist, was trying canvas caps and rubber face masks on the Sherpas to ensure a close fit.

The camera team from the BBC were setting up and checking their equipment.

Dr. David Peterson and I were supervising Sherpa Ang Tsering Namche and six of his friends, who were heaving huge boulders into position to make the walls of the hospital. The men sang and laughed at their labours and soon a village had mushroomed where a day before even the goraks had felt lonely.

CHAPTER 2

Mount Everest Base Camp. March 1971. "What the hell am I doing here?"
I ask myself. The answer lies a long time back.

In 1962 my wife, Sarah, and I drove overland to Nepal and worked at
Shanta Bhawan Hospital in Kathmandu for six months; I was doing a
residency mainly in general surgery while Sarah nursed in the children's
ward. This experience opened our eyes to new vistas of medicine and
introduced us, for the first time, to a wide variety of tropical diseases.
I learned to deal with many conditions that are seen by young doctors
only as illustrations of rarity or gross pathology in medical textbooks.
In my previously sheltered hospital training I had never encountered such
poverty and suffering. In Nepal a sick man was counted lucky if he had
to walk or be carried for only a week to reach a doctor. I learnt to make
do with limited facilities and laboratory investigations in the practice of
basic clinical medicine divorced from the sophistication to which I was
accustomed in a welfare state.

Learning to speak the Nepali language was perhaps the most important factor for my future. Each week Sarah and I had a one-hour lesson from a Nepali guru, who gave us the grammatical groundwork to build on; by frequently talking with patients our speaking improved and our understanding of the Nepali way of life grew. We treated patients from many parts of Nepal: Magars and Gurungs from the West; Newars and Brahmins of the Kathmandu Valley; Tamangs, Limbus and Rais from the East. A Tibetan refugee camp stood close by the hospital and about one third of all our work was concerned with these poor, dejected people who, at that time, were in a pathetic state, having recently been ejected from their homeland without money or possessions.

We made a few contacts with Sherpas through Colonel Jimmy Roberts and little did I imagine then that nine years later he would be one of my leaders on an expedition to Everest.

I had known about Jimmy for a long time, having read of his many journeys and climbs in the Himalayas. He fell in love with mountains as a boy and spent many holidays in the Alps before joining the Indian Army. Before the Second World War he made several forays into the Karakoram and western Himalayas, including an attempt on Masherbrum in 1938. In the war he moved from his own regiment, the 1st Gurkha Rifles, to join a Gurkha parachute regiment; during the Japanese offensive he was dropped into Burma and won the Military Cross. He was in an early climbing party allowed into Nepal in 1950, when he explored the country north of Annapurna and west of Himalchuli, with H.W. Tilman, Charles Evans and others. On the 1953 British Everest expedition he acted as a transport officer responsible for bringing up a convoy of a hundred porters with the oxygen equipment. On arrival at Base Camp John Hunt invited him to join the expedition, but he refused and went off to climb Mera Peak (23,000 feet, 6,900 metres) on his own. In the subsequent years he went many times to the west of Nepal, climbing peaks of the Dhaulagiri range, and in his wanderings all over the Nepal Himalayas he acquired as much knowledge of them as any other man.

He was appointed military attaché to the British Embassy in Kathmandu in 1958, a post he held until he told a visiting brigadier where to go, in unminced words. He was retired early as a lieutenant-colonel and settled into the stables of an old Rana palace to the north of the town, earning his living then by making postcards of the mountains; now he has set up a trekking business that flourishes and provides much steady work for the Sherpas. Visiting him for tea, we sat on empty orange-boxes round a table made of upturned tea chests. On a camp bed his clothes were laid out as for a military kit inspection. His Sherpa servants and dogs slept on reed mats in the kitchen. We had the feeling that at the sound of a bugle call they would all be ready to get up and march. He regularly sent me a short note by the hand of his Sherpas who would appear at the hospital on Wednesday afternoon leading two Labrador dogs; it read, "Please treat dogs and boys for worms. J.O.M.R." During our months in Kathmandu we got to know Jimmy better; he was a reserved man with hesitant speech who outwardly gave an appearance of brusqueness, but these barriers fell on acquaintance. His attitude to mountains was quite uncomplicated — he loved them deeply and chose to live among them for as much time as he could, observing the bird and animal life about which he had become an expert.

By strange chance, at that time in Kathmandu I met my other expedition leader-to-be — Norman Dyhrenfurth. During a party at the house of an American diplomat, I found my wife gazing fixedly at a well-groomed, bronzed and Grecian-god-like figure with a square, forceful jaw; who I discovered was to be the leader of the proposed American expedition to Mount Everest for the following year. His warmth and charm made a deep impression on us then and he has changed little since.

Norman Dyhrenfurth is a good mountaineer, a brilliant fundraiser, a polished speaker and performer in his own professional milieu in front of a moving camera. He is also a sound organizer of such a vastly complicated venture as a large Himalayan expedition. On the Swiss expedition to Lhotse in 1955 Norman was the climber in charge of all photography and five years later was again with the Swiss on Dhaulagiri I, when

Michel Vaucher was a fellow member. On an unsuccessful search for the Abominable Snowman in 1960, Norman travelled widely in the highlands of Nepal, often alone with only Sherpa companions. He speaks four languages fluently — English, French, German and Italian — and can switch with ease from one to another. I saw Norman occasionally while he was in Kathmandu in 1962 and then lost track of him till 1969.

After six months' work in Kathmandu, a month of which had been pleasantly spent at Tansen, a small peripheral country hospital four days' walk from Pokhara in the west, Sarah and I prepared our "expedition" to the Dhaulagiri range. To equip our two Sherpas and six Tamang coolies we raided the hospital's "missionary barrel" for old suits of pyjamas, gloves and gym shoes and gave every man a brightly coloured woolly bobble-cap lovingly knitted by some charitable women's league back in the United States. The Sherpas each had a blue boiler-suit for high-altitude wear. We set off from Pokhara for three months in the far west of Nepal with six porters, a marked contrast to the thousand we now had for Everest. We explored and mapped Hiunchuli Patan, a beautiful 19,500-foot (5,900-metre) mountain at the end of the Dhaulagiri chain. I crossed to the Barbung Khola in the north while Sarah returned with four of the coolies by the way we had come, as she was three months' pregnant and had an aversion to eating rice, our staple food, and the weather was becoming very cold and windy. I made a full circle round Dhaulagiri by crossing the Mu La to reach Jomossom. Leaving this place, after a visit to the pilgrimage shrine of Muktinath, I followed the Kali Gandaki River south to Pokhara and arrived two days later, having trotted most of the way since I was in a hurry to see my wife again.

We returned to England by way of Bangkok, Borneo and Hong Kong, and during the next year I took diplomas in obstetrics and anaesthetics. In 1964 I was asked to take charge of the International Grenfell Association flying doctor service for Northern Labrador, operating out of North West River, during the year's absence of the superintendent. I had already done six months' surgery at the main hospital in St. Anthony, Newfoundland, just after I qualified, so I knew the sort of conditions to expect.

The year in Labrador was one of the most rewarding and exciting of my medical life. Another doctor and myself operated on all the emergencies and fulfilled the posts of physician, radio operator, radiographer and laboratory technician. We came to learn how difficult the practice of medicine can be out in the bush with no one to fall back on for help. I travelled "down North on the Labrador" by air and boat, on snowshoe and by dog team, and developed a deep affection for that desolate land and its hardy breed of men, who are totally adapted to the extreme climate they live in.

In 1967, after some surgical exams, I followed up an invitation from the king of Bhutan, and with my wife and family, Adam aged three and a half and Judith aged eighteen months, travelled across the Bhutan Himalayas from west to east. We gathered twelve loads of equipment and, using ponies for transport, spent five months wandering across the country studying the prevalence of endemic goitre. We had a Bhutanese boy, Chimmi Wangchuck, as an assistant and a Darjeeling Sherpani ayah to help with the children. I did some climbing exploration on the northern border with Tibet and we travelled some little-known terrain of exceptional beauty.

Two years later I tried to return alone to Bhutan to follow up the results of my goitre study but found the doors barred for political reasons, so I went to East Nepal on a short adventure. Leaving Darjeeling with one Sherpa, I trekked in to the Everest region from Jaynagar on the southern border of Nepal.

On a brief visit to Kathmandu before this journey I met Michael Cheney, a partner with Jimmy Roberts in the mountain travel business that organized trekking parties in the Nepal Himalayas. He told me about plans for the international expedition to Mount Everest in 1971 and I raised my hands in horror at the size and magnitude of it.

"Jimmy's away shooting in Kashmir at the moment," said Mike, "but I know they are looking for a doctor."

"It doesn't sound at all my sort of outing, but if they want a jack-of-all-trades to sit at the bottom I might think about it," I said jokingly.

I left Mike Cheney to trek off into East Nepal and gave little further thought to our conversation.

On the march from the southern border, at the end of September, I caught the last of the monsoon and the sporadic storms that bear witness to the death throes of the rainy season, which ends with a bang of thunder about this time. We reached Namche Bazaar, the heart of Solu Khumbu and homeland of the Sherpas. I climbed a hill above the village from where I could look far up the two valleys that join in a ravine a thousand feet (three hundred metres) below. Over the roofs of Namche, northwestwards up the Bhote Kosi, two snow-clad peaks dominate the Nangpa La, the main trading pass to Tibet. Square white houses with low-pitched roofs of split pine slats stand one above the other on a terraced hillside amphitheatre and below them are potato fields and two chortens, half-domed religious shrines standing on five-tiered pedestals.

To the northeast a magnificent wide mountain panorama was laid out. In the centre of the group stands the high, featureless wall of Lhotse, over the crest of which appears a small conical summit — that of Everest itself. Clouds whipped by tempestuous winds are streaked into variegated tortuous patterns in the sky over the big mountains. Flanking this extraordinary centrepiece lay Taweche on my left and on my right Ama Dablam, Kangtega and Tamserku. Looking at the beautiful spire of Ama Dablam I felt an intense sadness as I remembered my friend George Fraser who, in 1961, disappeared on it within a few hundred feet of the top and was never seen again. He and his companion, Mike Harris, may have reached the top, but what a fearful price to pay for the glory.

From the base of Kangtega a long ridge takes a steeply inclined sweep towards the valley, levels out to green alp and then drops precipitously to the river gorge. On this level meadow stands Thyangboche Monastery, the tiered roofs of which are surmounted by the cupola of the gompa itself.

This peaceful scene of unique beauty was disturbed by the clamour of a thousand or more voices coming from a Japanese expedition moving off from their camp at Namche towards Everest. Men with long sections of aluminium ladder balanced clumsily on their backs jostled with others carrying large boxes numbered and marked with different-coloured paints in cryptic Japanese writing. Large bottles of liquid gas, canvas bags with tent poles projecting from them, long logs to be used for bridging crevasses and all the elaborate paraphernalia of expedition life were loaded onto the backs of porters: Tibetans with gold-embroidered flower-pot hats with the peaks either tucked under or hanging over an ear or an eyebrow, ruddy-cheeked Sherpani girls with dirty towel squares on their heads to ease the weight of the headband that supports most of the load. Ambling yaks with long hairy coats and bells with red tassels round their necks, carrying loads strapped either side of a wooden pack saddle, jostled with one another.

Shouting orders to this melee were several well-dressed Sherpas with smart white peaked caps and lightly filled yellow rucksacks, for all the world the new-generation Himalayan equivalent of the Alpine guides. Watching this activity from the sidelines were a number of gentlemen with noticeably similar features to the Sherpas but festooned with every type of camera and, like extravagant hunters, shooting everything that crossed their view.

"So this is an expedition," I said to myself derisively. "A horde of men disturbing the peace and devouring the land like locusts." In Afghanistan I had seen the sun darkened by a swarm, so this was no idle analogy.

I sat in a flat meadow where edelweiss and many tiny gentians grew and the scarlet leaves of a dying plant added a splash of colour to the fore-ground. I watched this miniature army advancing along the level moun-tain path that traverses the gullies of the hill between where I was and Thyangboche on the other side of the valley. As they moved off at their pace I turned and continued at mine; one Sherpa, one rucksack, no tent, no food; the bare essentials were provided by the land we moved through, at a speed that was of our own choosing and in directions sought on the flight of fancy.

Dorje and I spent the next two weeks exploring the valleys beyond Thyangboche and climbed Pokalde (19,500 feet, 5,900 metres), a peak above Dingboche. We returned to Phortse and passed a further week walking towards the foot of Cho Oyu. Finally we came back to the hospital at Kunde, having lost a lot of weight and in great need of a shower.

I was sitting on the balcony of the hospital, built by Sir Edmund Hillary for the Sherpas of Khumbu, looking out over the wooden roofs of Kunde and Khumjung to the magnificent towering peak of Ama Dablam and two other 23,000-foot (6,900-metre) peaks, Kangtega and Tamserku. Quite unexpectedly Barry Bishop, who had reached the summit of Everest with the Americans in 1963, arrived with a rucksack on his back and a shovel on his shoulder. He was currently occupied on a geographical thesis in West Nepal, where he was living with his family for a year. He thrust a hand forward and beamed.

"You're going to Everest, Peter. Great news."

I was staggered. Barry continued, "I met Norman and Jimmy in Kathmandu and they discussed the doctor business and decided you fit the bill."

"But I didn't even ask to go," I said feebly. "I was only joking with Mike Cheney. How can I accept when I haven't even discussed it with Sarah?"

"Don't worry," said Barry, "Norman is trekking in to Namche in two days' time so you can meet him there and ask about it."

I slept little that night, turning the whole exciting prospect over in my mind. I knew the dangers of Everest. Barry had come to bury his friend Jake Breitenbach, whose body had just been found in the Icefall after lying for six years under the moving glacier. I knew of the mystique and prestige attached to the mountain. I knew how I had scorned the idea of big expeditions. But I also knew that an invitation like this was going to be difficult to refuse and would never come my way again.

Two days later I met Norman Dyhrenfurth at the Namche Bazaar police post where he had just arrived with his wife and a group of friends, having walked from Kathmandu. Norman looked fit and bursting with energy and enthusiasm while his wilting party sat nursing blistered feet, sunburnt noses and cramps in their bellies.

He took my hand in a vice-like grip and in affable American style greeted me.

"Hi, Peter, great to see you again." He then came straight to the point with no meandering. "I've just been in Kathmandu discussing the international expedition with Jimmy Roberts. We've had a lot of applications for the doctor's job but we like your record."

"Just tell me a little about what you're after," I said.

"Sure," replied Norman. "We want a doctor with wide medical experience and if possible with knowledge of the Himalayas who will take charge as far as Advance Base Camp. He must be a climber, but definitely with no aspirations to go high on the mountain. We're going to have another climbing doctor who can do any work on the Face."

"That sounds all right. I certainly don't want to stick my neck out," I said. "But I can't give you an answer till I've discussed it with my wife."

"Can you let me know by January 1st?" asked Norman.

"Okay. January 1st." I felt relieved. They had other applicants so I had the time and scope for honourable refusal if I wished to decline, after more logical deliberation when I had come down to earth again; and anyway they might not select me.

I wrote a letter to Sarah straightaway:

I felt very honoured to have even been considered let alone asked. If it were just another expedition, I know I would not be interested. There will probably never be an expedition like this again and at worst for two months' boredom sitting at Base Camp, or at best for a fascinating medical experience, it would be a remarkable team to have been part of. I just don't know, my love. Let's think a lot about it. I hardly even know if I want to go myself.

On my return to England I looked for persons whom I could consult. While I was in Caernarvonshire I visited Sir Charles Evans, later the vice-chancellor of Bangor University, who had narrowly missed being the first man on top of Everest in 1953. He and Tom Bourdillon had been forced to turn back from the South Summit when their oxygen system froze up.

He was a Himalayan explorer of the widest experience and also a surgeon, although on Everest he was not the expedition doctor. He helped me to view the problem from every angle — my career, the job itself, large international expeditions, the dangers involved. But most of all he dwelled on the latter.

"The Icefall is a dangerous place," he said, "and I'm not sure it's justified if you're only going up into the Cwm to be doctor at Advance Base without a chance of climbing the mountain."

Charles Evans was no man to turn down an adventure lightly and I was surprised at his cautious approach. He went on: "But I suppose if you consider the thousands of individual journeys that have been made through the Icefall in half a dozen or more major expeditions it's surprising how few accidents there have been. If you put the figures in the hands of an actuary he'd probably lay pretty good odds against an accident. Taken all in all I think you should go."

Eric Shipton came down to stay with us in Bristol. We went for a long walk in the woods overlooking the Avon gorge and became quite lost, much to the amusement of my son Adam, who thought that so famous an explorer had no right to lose his way in rural England.

I knew that Eric's view would balance any over-enthusiasm for the project on my part. He never made a secret of his contempt for large unwieldy parties, although he himself took part in the 1933, 1935, 1936 and 1938 expeditions to Everest from the north side by way of Tibet. His forte had been small, lightly equipped teams moving through unknown country and climbing small peaks. His philosophy was one I have always admired and tried to follow.

At the end of two hours' discussion we had covered every conceivable pro and con and the majority was con. Big expeditions are hell: they are expensive, people squabble, you never properly see the country you are passing through. We talked about the motives for going to Everest, and Eric said, "To the non-climbing public it is THE mountain and a good deal of kudos falls on anyone going on an Everest expedition. This does no harm and who can tell what good it may bring? There's no point in pretending we don't all enjoy some limelight; it's part of the whole business."

Finally we had chewed over all the old arguments and there seemed little more to say. Everything was against going. Suddenly Eric said, "Well, I think you should go. It may be hell; don't expect to enjoy it. It could be interesting; with such a big party someone's bound to get sick. And it's not every day you get asked to go to Everest."

"You're right, Eric," I said, and went to bed knowing that the decision had been made. I talked it over with Sarah, my final arbiter, who said, "Yes, darling, you must accept it." And so I went to sleep, but it was an uneasy sleep.

In January I received an "expedition letter," the first of many similar, lengthy documents.

"… list of expedition members. To these are now added Dr. Peter Steele of England as Senior M.O. who will face the considerable challenge … of keeping Sherpas and sahibs healthy and moderately happy up to and including Advance Base."

Before I came on the scene some abrasive correspondence had been conducted between an American doctor, appointed as "oxygen expert, high-altitude physician and climber," and the leaders — as a "senior" doctor was to be appointed, did this mean he would be the "junior" doctor? Was it thought his qualifications were not good enough? If so, he would have to reconsider his position.

I wrote a letter to the expedition leaders.

Before either you or I make a final decision on the matter of a "second doctor" for the 1971 expedition, I feel certain points must be clarified. From your circular and from reports on certain correspondence with Dr. — I gather that he would like to be involved in climbing on the Face, organizing the oxygen programme and supervising medicine at the base. This would seem to me a very full whole-time job, and I do not really see where another doctor would fit in. If you do want a doctor at Advance Base camp it seems that the ultimate responsibility for decisions on the health of the party should rest with him, for reasons that I do not need to enlarge on.

I have discussed this matter with Charles Evans and Michael Ward who are both adamant on the ultimate responsibility of the work resting in the hands of the Advance Base doctor. I am not in the least concerned about "status" and what the Advance Base doctor is called does not worry me, but obviously there is some problem from this angle and I would frankly be very reluctant to get involved in a squabble with another doctor over status which could be disastrous and quite out of the interests of any sick member of the team.

Shortly afterwards I heard that Dr. David Peterson, then working in the U.S.A., had been taken on as the Face-climbing doctor in place of the other member, who had withdrawn.

I set to work ordering the medical supplies. The problem that faced me was how to select enough aspirins, one-inch bandages, artery clips and so on for seventy men (a team of thirty members and forty Sherpas) for four months in order to deal with anything from a pain in the toe to a serious head injury needing a hole to be drilled in the skull.

First I sat down and wrote a list of all the things I thought we would need, categorized under systems, e.g., gastrointestinal drugs, dressings, skin creams, surgical instruments, antibiotics, anaesthetic equipment; all the time trying to imagine being on this God-forsaken moraine with help a couple of hundred miles away and someone in the expedition seriously sick. Against this yardstick every item was measured. Where one drug would suffice I did not duplicate with different brands; where one bandage or dressing would fulfil more than one purpose I chose it. Before finalizing the list of my own requirements I wrote to the doctors of some recent large expeditions asking for copies of their equipment inventories to compare with my own.

Then I wrote to the drug manufacturers, or rather, since Norman had told me "by all means use a secretary," I got my boss's daughter to write the letters. Every firm responded generously and I was able to reassure them that nothing would be wasted, as I had arranged with Sir Edmund Hillary to leave any drugs remaining at the end of the expedition with the doctor at Kunde Hospital.

At the time I was working in the Plastic Surgery Unit of Frenchay Hospital, Bristol, and I managed to appropriate a storeroom off one of the wards for my "Aladdin's Cave." Packages began to arrive daily and it was just like Christmas again, unwrapping parcel after parcel.

By December, after nine months of preparation, the task was complete, and as I saw the last box go into the crates ready for shipping to India I heaved a sigh of deep relief. If I had forgotten anything now there was little I could do about it and I had only myself to blame.

But as the date approached for the expedition to leave Europe I grew more and more apprehensive about the whole venture and doubts crowded in on me. I would wake in the early hours of the morning and think till day broke about the responsibility I had to carry and the dangers that might come my way. The responsibility not only involved having to be ready to deal with any eventuality in the field of medicine or surgery but also that of possibly having to advise one of the world's top climbers, poised and eager to go for the top, that I thought he should go down; the dangers centred mainly round the Icefall.

Many times I thought over my talk with Charles Evans, and every book I read about Everest told gloomy stories of the Icefall and had horrific pictures, naturally of the most spectacular and contorted parts of it. I was especially worried by a photo in a glossy colour folder of the previous year's Japanese expedition, that I took care to hide from Sarah. A large number of men of both the Japanese Alpine Club and the ski team were standing in a circle with their heads bowed; in the centre, wrapped in tarpaulin, were the bodies of six Sherpas killed in an accident in the Icefall. I could not get it out of my mind and had nightmares of self reproach for agreeing to go. Too many wives of my friends had met early widowhood and I had seen the effect this had on their children. My parents died when I was a child and I suffered much because of it, so why should I risk doing the same to my own children?

I worried myself into such a state that I was getting dyspeptic stomach pains and I even wondered if I would be fit to go on the expedition. But it was now too late to withdraw honourably. One evening I poured out all my fears to my friend Ian Taylor, an Australian plastic surgeon working with me and a man of jovial and equable personality. He listened attentively and gave me the quiet encouragement I needed. From that day my stomach ache disappeared and I started to sleep better. I learnt an important lesson about the powers of psychosomatic medicine from this experience.

A "shakedown" meeting had been planned to take place in Europe in the autumn for all members, but as the expedition was passing through one of its recurrent financial crises the meeting had to be abandoned. As I would be unable to do the medical examinations personally I sent a letter to each member.

There are certain essential checks that need to be done and I would be grateful if each of you would see to it at the earliest possible opportunity and let me have the results.

1. *Blood Group. You should have your blood group tested at a reliable laboratory and have a card with all details written on it in your possession; at the same time it would be wise to check your haemoglobin.*
2. *Chest x-ray. Only the report should be sent to me. You should have a recent Mantoux test for tb and if this is negative b.c.g. inoculation is advisable.*
3. *Inoculations. You should obtain written certificates to the effect that you have had the essential ones done, these are: smallpox, cholera, typhoid, paratyphoid a and b, tetanus, polio.*
4. *Full Urinalysis.*
5. *Dental Check. As fillings tend to become loose in the cold.*
6. *Piles. Anyone with a suspicion of piles should have treatment, as piles tend to get very much worse at altitude and can be a problem.*
7. *Please would you let me know of any notable illness you have had in the past and whether you suffer from any drug sensitivity.*

I had some amusing replies written in better English than I could have managed in their respective languages. Odd Eliassen wrote, "By the way I can tell you that I smashed two fingers on the right hand ... with a sledge hammer. They were both broken in different piesis. I do really hope that they will be good again till we arrived in Kathmandu." They were. Leo Schlömmer was more succinct, "My body is O.K." Wolfgang Axt had suggestions for pills to help acclimatization that they had used in the Hindu Kush. The French-speakers thought, with good reason, that "piles" meant batteries.

Don Whillans ran into difficulty when he presented himself at the local Blood Transfusion Centre, asking for his blood group to be tested. After an hour of debate the two elderly ladies behind the desk said with finality, "We can only do your blood grouping for a five pound fee, Mr. Whillans. Otherwise you can have it tested at the hospital through your own doctor."

Don left them in dudgeon, muttering in the language of Lancashire. A hundred yards down the road he heard the commissionaire calling him back.

"Excuse me, sir, but the ladies upstairs would like to see you again."

Don reluctantly returned.

"Mr. Whillans, we've thought of a way round this problem. If you would care to sign your heart and lungs away we can do your blood group."

"Bloody cobblers!" exploded Don. "By the time I've finished with 'em you'll have a long way to go to collect 'em." He submitted to the test, got his card and disappeared in a cloud of anger.

As one might expect, little else of note came out of the medical preliminaries since I was dealing with a group of men in first-class physical condition.

However, three days before leaving Europe, Norman Dyhrenfurth was diagnosed as having an obscure and rare disease of the thyroid gland called Hashimoto's autoimmune thyroiditis. He had been feeling tired for a month or two — hardly surprising considering the monumental task of launching the expedition and dealing with almost daily financial crises.

He had palpitations of the heart and night sweats and his physician discovered an enlarged thyroid gland, from which a little piece was taken by a needle for biopsy examination. He had been started on treatment with steroids and thyroid gland extract and was already improving. He had written to me in an earlier letter, "Even if I'm dying of TB I'm still coming to Everest after all this work!" Who was I to challenge that?

I took the rather casual attitude that people must be fairly fit to consider going to Everest. I did not want to be pedantic about medicals as so many expeditions have been in the past, to the exclusion of many good and suitable men. I was prepared to cope with most medical problems and if anyone was hiding a secret it was he who took the risk. If Scott had carefully assessed Edward Wilson's past medical record he would never have taken him to the South Pole, as he had been a sickly youth, having suffered from tuberculosis. Scott and the world would have been immeasurably the poorer for the lack of Wilson's medical skill, his memoirs of inspiring courage, his warm personality and his watercolour paintings and drawings of birds.

CHAPTER 3

During the march-in I got to know Ang Tsering, the Sherpa assigned to help in the medical work. He was short and handsome, polite and unfailingly cheerful.

I had travelled with some good Sherpas before and had tried to live with them on an equal footing to avoid the utterly sterile sahib-Sherpa relationship of many large expeditions. But over a period of several weeks' close contact it is rare not to have some disagreements. However, working for four months with Ang Tsering, I found him a pleasant companion who showed astonishing aptitude as a medical assistant.

Ang Tsering was a true Tibetan, having been born, like Tenzing Norgay of 1953 Everest fame, in a village on the north side of the Nangpa La in Tibet. But in the days before the Chinese invasion and oppression there was regular trade and exchange between the two sides of the Himalayan divide regardless of political boundaries and frontiers; a throne was reserved beside the altar of Thyangboche Gompa for the High

Lama of Rongbuk Monastery in Tibet for use on his occasional pastoral visits when he crossed the mountains into Nepal.

Ang Tsering's father was a trader and several times took the boy to Lhasa on business. Then the family moved south and settled in Namche, the most cosmopolitan bazaar in the region. Ang Tsering went to school in Namche before Sir Edmund Hillary's school-building program had really begun to raise the standard of education in the Khumbu (in 1971 a Sherpa boy topped the list in the school-leaving certificates for the whole of Nepal). But Ang Tsering's intelligence and astuteness were able to flourish and he read English books and wrote and did accounts for his less-educated friends.

He spent a year and a half with Barry Bishop, who was engaged on a geographical study of the Jumla region of West Nepal. He married a Gurung wife during this time and had brought her and their baby out east to live with his family, not an easy situation for her as she was living with in-laws of a different racial group.

During clinics on the approach march I had the opportunity to teach Ang Tsering to do dressings, give injections and dispense treatments. He was keen to learn and rarely needed to be shown more than once how to do some new procedure.

With my fellow physician, David Peterson, we made up the medical team for the expedition. Dave had been qualified as a doctor for a year and was working on a thesis on high-altitude physiology.

He was a man of gigantic size, six and a half feet tall and weighing nearly two hundred pounds; he peered out through round spectacles, his face framed by a long curly beard and moustache and hair that hung down the back of his neck, round which were some coloured beads. He had proved himself a strong climber on many mountains of the United States, especially in the Grand Teton group. A devotee of the peace movement, he had the ban-the-bomb sign drawn on his equipment and this motif was the insignia on a ring he wore.

His medical inexperience was balanced by enthusiasm and he found my more phlegmatic Anglo-Saxon approach hard to reconcile. My inclination, when faced with a patient complaining of minor symptoms, is to put him to bed with an aspirin and review the situation after he has slept a little, instead of starting treatment immediately. Some people thought my approach rather casual, but I was determined not to encourage too deep a dependence on the doctors because, for long periods of time, they might be on their own and would need to be accustomed to fend for themselves.

I was glad that expedition members had a choice of whom they could consult for medical advice as this is a very personal matter. Some will like the approach of one doctor and not that of another, purely on personality, and consulting someone you do not like will never be satisfactory, however sound his or her medicine.

David Peterson and I were rarely in the same place at the same time as I was intentionally trying to keep the medical work as widely spaced as possible and available to many people. This prevented any diversity of our views from causing too much conflict, which was always a danger if we were on top of each other for long.

During the march-in (February 28 to March 23) we held clinics for the Sherpas and porters each evening soon after arriving in camp. Ang Tsering gathered the aluminium boxes marked with a red cross on all sides for easy identification. One box was filled with dressings, bandages, plaster of Paris and Elastoplast; another held the medicines, pills, creams and crystals in self-sealing plastic picnic boxes which made packing easier. Emergency equipment was kept in different boxes that always travelled with us and could be opened if the occasion demanded. But we tried to work out of two boxes only, since the less unpacking and repacking on the march the easier it was.

Ang Tsering would summon the patients and we appointed a fourteen-year-old coolie, Pasang Wangchuk, a cheeky boy with a winning smile, to be our policeman and to line up those attending the clinic into manageable order.

We usually camped outside villages for convenience and to avoid pilfering. Not many casual callers came and I specifically intended not to treat the local population, a policy which may seem hard-hearted in a country where medical facilities are scarce, but I mistrust peripatetic medicine. It is easy to set up roadside clinics, in the accepted fashion of expeditions, to hand out pills to lines of waiting patients on the strength of spot diagnoses and to move on next day. This does little lasting good, as people will swap or trade their pills with friends — a red for a brown one, or two rupees for a couple of white tablets — and it may do positive harm.

THE PERMANENT DOCTORS scattered sparsely across the country are continually waging war against suspicion of modern medicine, superstition handed down through generations and quack medicine practised by witch doctors and lamas. The fight is uphill and the rewards are small. An outsider flashing by and handing out medicines as a panacea puts entirely the wrong face on the problem and uneducated people come to expect that one-shot treatment is the answer to their ills.

When I saw patients on the road I tried to send them on to the nearest doctor with a note about their condition. Over the years, medical facilities in Nepal have improved greatly and now dispensaries and doctors are to be found at distances of not more than a day or two's travelling.

Education about the benefits of modern medicine is a long-term matter and should proceed hand in hand with existing facilities. To the uninitiated there is something exciting about seeing a hundred people queuing up for the hand of the healer, but I feel this temptation must be resisted in the interests of the future. Without speaking the language a doctor can do little but make a cursory appraisal of the problem.

On the march-in the most common complaints of the porters were coughs aggravated by excessive smoking of noxious herbal mixtures, and a variety of non-specific aches in muscles and feet caused by carrying excessive loads. A porter is paid a fee of ten rupees to carry a basic weight of sixty-fix pounds (thirty kilograms) for six to eight hours each day, but he will probably have a further twenty pounds (ten kilograms) of his own personal belongings, bedding and food on top of this. Wages have tripled during the nine years since I first went to Nepal.

Many of the Sherpa porters were women and there were a few teenage children among them. All provide their own food and sleep in the open round wood fires.

During the night at Gorak Shep on the way up to Base Camp some yaks were grazing on the steep hill above our tents. One of them dislodged a boulder that rolled down the hill picking up speed as it went. I half awoke and heard a bumpety-bump sound and then a thud followed by cries and wailing. I had become so used to the nocturnal shouts of men fighting over their women that I paid little heed at first. But as the noise continued I pulled on some clothes and crawled out into the moonlight. Barely three yards from my tent I saw a woman lying on blankets moaning, and beside her was a boulder weighing about forty-five pounds (twenty kilograms). On examining her I found that five ribs had been fractured by the stone. Had she been hit on the head she might have died and I realized that my own head had not been far away, so after that incident I always placed my tin trunk at the head end of my tent if any such danger were remotely possible. I strapped up the woman's chest, gave her some pain-killing drugs and sent her off home. I later heard that she had completely recovered. I treated the porters when necessary, but when it was evident their visits were made solely out of curiosity I gave a placebo without any twinge of conscience. Ang Tsering made up solutions of different-coloured crystals and would paint the affected areas — gentian violet, mercurochrome orange and brilliant green. These colours gained the reputation of powerful fertility rejuvenators and aphrodisiacs and had I been in commercial medicine I would have made a small fortune. With any placebo we always gave a multivitamin pill that we knew could do nothing but good; these were gathered from many different firms, came in many different shapes and ranged through every colour of the rainbow.

Nepalis love inunctions to rub into parts of the body afflicted with pain. I took the precaution of bringing a large supply of Iodex ointment scented with wintergreen, which required a lot of hard rubbing to remove the dark stain yet left behind a delicious, fresh smell. This worked wonders on tired muscles and aching joints, and was in steady demand.

Illnesses among the expedition members on the march-in were not severe, though often quite debilitating. It was a time of gentle ambling through beautiful foothills among the finest mountain scenery in the world, so the stresses were not too great. Vague aches and pains racked the limbs of the less fit and more overweight members of the party. "Malish," or ointment, was prescribed liberally and usually with success. You may well ask why people setting off for Everest were unfit and over-weight. Why hadn't they trained?

I think training for a Himalayan expedition is of doubtful advantage. Given a basic fitness without which a member would not be considered for selection, training starts at Kathmandu; if a person cannot get fit in three weeks of walking across the grain of the country, crossing passes of 12,000 feet (3,700 metres) and descending to valleys at 4,000 feet (1,200 metres), he or she never will do so.

Indeed, being well covered before you start may prove an asset. The lean ones like Dougal Haston, Leo Schlömmer and myself could only get leaner — a physical quality of little benefit under rigorous cold. The heavier ones, like Michel Vaucher, Carlo Mauri and Toni Hiebeler, soon slimmed down with exercise. Murray Sayle became quite sylph-like.

If you go into rigid training before reaching Nepal, the fitness soon wears off while packing and sitting around Kathmandu for two weeks. The inevitable bout of diarrhea will undo a few weeks' vigorous exercise in as many hours. Dave Peterson, who had clanked around Kathmandu with anklets loaded with five pounds of lead shot, shed them early in the march as he lost fluid and weight rapidly after gut-rot set in.

Tired arms and a condition know medically as "frozen shoulder" developed with the use of expedition umbrellas. Umbrellas are essential equipment for Himalayan mountaineers; even the poorest coolie will possess one. They are on sale in every marketplace, made of rough black cloth with a long, curved bamboo handle that can be hooked into a ruck-sack strap to avoid the bother of holding it in the hand; in emergency they are strong enough to use for braking on a snow or scree glissade, like an ice axe. The best quality cost less than a dollar and can be bought at any market stall across the country. Ours were from Europe, short-handled, of bright red plastic and more suited to a lady on an expensive shopping spree.

Blisters were a common trouble before feet became hardened and Dr. Dave Peterson made attending to them his special business. If a blister was unbroken he burst the water bubble with a sterile needle and removed any dead skin. Then the raw area was sprayed with compound tincture of benzoin, which stimulated the healing and also a lot of sensitive pain endings. Finally an adhesive Elastoplast dressing or an orthopaedic felt corn pad was applied.

The most tiresome malady of the early days was the diarrhea that seems inevitable for Europeans soon after arriving in the East. The gut appears to react violently to unaccustomed bacteria and takes a little while to make friends with its new flora. Fourteen members had diarrhea requiring treatment and six had two or more attacks.

I compounded a very powerful "blunderbuss cocktail" that rarely failed to cure the problem in one dose. The recipe was as follows: two tablespoons of kaolin powder; between two and twenty Lomotil tablets, depending on the severity of the attack and the response to treatment (this medicine was given to the American astronauts to stop them getting nervous runs on re-entry); codeine phosphate, thirty milligrams (a wonderful drug useful for pain, cough or diarrhea and quite indispensable in a medical pack); finally tincture of morphine (chlorodyne), four drops by day or six drops at night, as it is a powerful sleep-inducing drug.

One member came to me for a cocktail at our acclimatization camp at Pheriche and, though he should have known better, set off to attempt a gully climb that Dougal Haston and I had done the day before. He fell asleep at the bottom of the first pitch, and was lucky that he had climbed no higher or he would have had to be lowered off. He was most indignant that I had spoiled his climb.

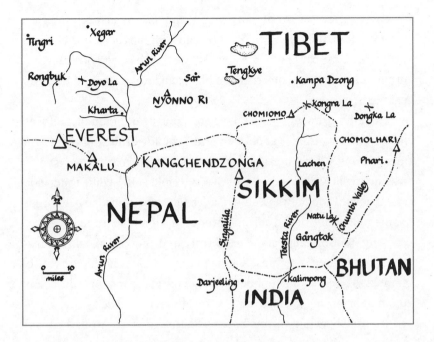

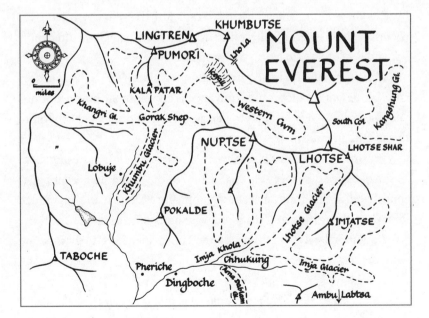

After the exclusion of worms and amoebae by inspection of the patient's stool, if diarrhea did not clear up with the cocktail and if fever was present, the cause was presumed to be due to a bacterial infection. An antibiotic such as neomycin or sulphaguanidine was then added to the regime in full doses.

Parasites growing in the bowel are a plague of oriental countries; the commoner varieties are hookworms, roundworms, pinworms and threadworms. Children particularly suffer from them and when my wife was nursing in Kathmandu she once saw a child with a white thing in its nose that she thought was a stomach feeding-tube someone had forgotten to remove. She pulled at it and produced a roundworm 18 inches (46 cm) long. Worms cause anemia, diarrhea and abdominal pain that can mimic appendicitis so closely that the inexperienced doctor will be tempted to operate. But an inflamed appendix is as rare in India as it is common in Europe, owing mainly to the difference in diet.

No members had worms but two Sherpas suffered from them and were cured with doses of a foul-tasting green powder called Alcopar. In 1922 General Bruce took leave of Frank Smythe who was leaving for Everest with this sterling farewell, "Good luck my man, look after yourself and don't forget to worm your porters."

A nastier parasite to acquire is amoeba histolytica, which causes amoebic dysentery. Blood and slimy mucus appear in the bowel motions and the worm is very difficult to get rid of. A new drug has been found that is now an effective treatment.

Pruritis ani or itchy bottom troubled three persons suffering from severe diarrhea. I suspect the coarseness of the expedition toilet paper contributed to this annoyance, but by applying a cream with some added local anaesthetic the awful irritation was soothed.

National characteristics began to emerge in members' preoccupation with their bowels. In my letter home I wrote,

During my breakfast five people came separately to confide in me the state of their intestines and the length, consistence and colour of their morning motion.

I decided in future to eat on my own at a safe distance. I am trying to strike a happy medium between not being too indulgent towards minor ailments yet giving adequate reassurance and sympathy when needed. Some of the boys are very concerned with themselves, others are more phlegmatic.

The Europeans were particularly concerned with their regularity. From the hinterland of my schoolboy German I thought up the morning greeting, "*Gute Reise, gute Scheisse*" ["good trip, good shit"], which had Toni Hiebeler convulsed with mirth. He promised to adopt it as the motto for the Everest edition of his mountaineering periodical *Alpinismus*; it was particularly pertinent on the march-in, as poor Toni had bad dysentery that must have made him feel exceedingly miserable and which he bore with fortitude.

After one member succumbed to an attack of agonizing renal colic due to a stone in his ureter I wrote,

The Americans expect to be told at the dinner table every detail of the patient's condition, the anatomy, physiology, pathology, etc. in the same manner as they followed every T-wave of Eisenhower's electrocardiogram after his heart attack. Frankly I consider this a confidential matter to be discussed with the leaders alone.

In a hot climate much water is lost as sweat from the skin and vapour from the lungs; if, owing to diarrhea, significant loss occurs from the bowel, dehydration can rapidly set in. In these circumstances a daily fluid intake of five to seven litres may be necessary, which is a big volume of water to drink. I constantly had to nag those with diarrhea to drink and drink, because frequently they were vomiting at the same time.

A group of minor complaints also occurred during the march-in period. Colds were common and in two persons went on to sinusitis. An agonizing pain over the eyes gets worse every time you bend to do up a pair of bootlaces so you think your head will burst open. Running noses caused some bother, but we were fortunate in having plenty of paper handkerchiefs that were a blessing throughout the expedition.

Ear problems were scarce. One person suffered with otitis media, or inflammation of the ear drum, that quickly settled down on treatment with cortisone steroid drops; another had small polyps that became red and painful.

Soon after Don Whillans arrived he was troubled with dizziness, a condition he had had since childhood that comes on (while he is acclimatizing) at the start of every expedition. He understood his own problem and knew that when he had such an attack he would feel giddy and tend to fall towards the affected left ear, which became deaf; he would then have to lie down until it passed off. This condition of dizziness is very unpleasant during its short duration. Antihistamine tablets helped to curtail it and after two weeks the symptoms disappeared, as they had done during his expedition to Annapurna. This was fortunate, as vertigo on the Face of Mount Everest would not be healthy.

Tongues readily became sore and cracked, possibly aggravated by our diet being low in vitamin C. Gentian violet was helpful but unpopular as it left the patient looking like a painted circus clown with bright purple lips and stained teeth. But this good old-fashioned medicine is a wonderful healer of lesions on any mucous membrane surface.

Lips became easily sunburnt and the cracking, crusting and slow-healing ulceration caused much discomfort and became worse above the snowline with the reflection of the strong ultraviolet light. Sunburn troubled those who were not sufficiently cautious or respectful of the glare, which becomes more intense the higher one climbs. Protection by sun hats was important; Yvette Vaucher had a floppy yellow towelling hat with flowers on it, Carlo Mauri a jungle hat from his New Guinea travels, Dave Peterson a wide-brimmed felt Homburg, Wolfgang Axt a white cyclist's cap with a green transparent visor peak, Gary Colliver a Mexican straw hat, while Reizo Ito had one with frilly edges that tied with a bow under his chin.

Pubic lice irritated three members, who came to me with the telltale track of red bite marks round the lower abdomen where the beast had eaten its way relentlessly. DDT powder and medicated shampoo cleared them away quickly but the itching remained for a long while. In Bhutan my family discovered that parasitic infestations had a strange sex preference. Fleas attacked my son and me, while the girls always suffered from head lice, but the situation was never reversed.

Healing was much slower in the mountains and became worse the higher we climbed. Scrupulous care had to be given to cuts, insect bites and blisters to avoid their becoming infected.

WHEN WE ARRIVED at Base Camp it was a pleasure to be able to unpack our tin trunks and lay out the medicines, making dispensing easier.

The Base Camp hospital was built in the course of one morning. Ang Tsering supervised the construction with six other Sherpas who manhandled large moraine boulders into an acceptable rectangular pen measuring ten feet by eighteen feet with walls three feet high. The two end walls were built up into gables and between them was placed a large log that had been carried up for use in bridging crevasses. The roof of bonded polythene sheeting was slung over this centre beam and secured outside the walls by guy ropes.

As soon as we had walls and a roof over our heads Ang Tsering set to work on the interior. Two beds made of flat stones raised six inches off the floor were set at opposite corners and covered with foam mattresses. Empty food boxes made of strong, waxed cardboard were placed on their sides along one wall below the roof. These provided open cupboards in which we laid out our stock medicines. Against the wall, below them, stood the aluminium boxes holding the anaesthetic and surgical equipment that would only be required in an emergency.

On the opposite wall more boxes were arranged, and the floor was covered with cardboard several layers thick to keep out the damp of the melting glacier and to smooth the rocky surface. Using empty oxygen cases Ang Tsering built a desk with a wooden top, that turned writing from a chore into a pleasure. This desk could easily be moved into the centre of the floor to be used as an operating table if the occasion arose.

The possibility of a major accident caused me the most concern in planning for all the eventualities of such an expedition. In a fall, people could break bones which would need to be reduced and set; they could be hit on the head by falling rock that might cause bleeding inside the skull, which would have to be opened to let out the blood; they could damage their chests by fracturing ribs and so allow air to enter, with subsequent collapse of a lung requiring drainage; the spleen or bladder could be ruptured by a blow, for which an urgent operation would be necessary.

I did not fancy dealing with any of these major problems with our limited facilities, but they were an ever-present threat. I had brought a full "general set" of instruments that are standard for any operation and in addition I had some neurosurgical instruments for drilling holes in the head.

Anaesthesia under these conditions would be even more alarming than surgery. I had done a fair amount of anaesthetics in the past and so the techniques were familiar, but the behaviour of different agents at altitude is not well known and many physiological problems are caused by the thinness of the air and the scarcity of oxygen.

A self-inflating bag could be used to pump air into a patient's lungs or be connected to a cylinder to administer oxygen under positive pressure. I had taken advice on the simplest forms of anaesthetic for use in field conditions. An Oxford Miniature Vaporizer was chosen to give Trilene or Penthrane as an inhalational anaesthetic. I had used Ketamine, a new drug that can be given intramuscularly or directly into a vein, with success on burned patients to give anaesthesia for painful dressings; this drug seemed to have a real place in the sort of emergency I was likely to meet, when I might find myself completely alone and managing both ends of the patient at once.

I was given heart by recalling an operation that I had done in 1962 when I was in West Nepal under even less sophisticated circumstances.

ONE CHILLY MORNING late in October I had been walking beside the Barbung Khola north of Dhaulagiri with two Sherpas, Lakpa and Dakya.

Shafts of sunlight were breaking through the pine trees and throwing up steam from the frosty leaves. We left the forest and came into an open meadow where some ponies were grazing around an encampment of yak-hair tents. I had not intended to stop but as we were passing two worried-looking Tibetan men, their hair plaited and tied in pink ribbon and wearing sheepskin coats with ankle-long sleeves, emerged and asked if I would see a sick man in their tent. Lakpa and I entered while Dakya waited outside to stop Babu and Sahila, our Tamang coolies, who were following with the loads.

Inside the tent squatted several moaning relatives whom we moved outside to give us breathing room in the already confined space. In the middle of the floor a very sick young man of about twenty-five years was lying beside a wood fire, the smoke from which rose through a hole in the roof of the tent. On the far side of the tent, sitting cross-legged and Buddha-like, a handsome Tibetan lama wearing the purple and yellow robes of his office was telling his beads with a serene air, his mind high above the terrestrial commotion.

I paid my respects and learnt that he was a very senior Buddhist abbot, the Tara Gompa Lama, who was returning from a visit to the Dalai Lama, in exile in India. The sick man lived at Tarakot, a village we had passed the previous day; he was driving a herd of goats carrying salt from the north when he had fallen ill and called on the lama for help.

I turned to the Tarakot man and asked for his story. He had been quite well until a day and a half before when he suddenly became feverish with severe stomach pain and he had not passed urine or faeces since. He looked shocked and was a ghastly ashen colour. I examined his belly and found a tense, tender swelling the size of an egg in his right groin. Hearing no bowel sounds in his abdomen confirmed my opinion that his intestines were strangulated in the rupture. This means that a knuckle of bowel has slid down into the sac of an inguinal hernia, the neck of which is so tight that it cuts off the blood supply; unless this is relieved soon, the bowel becomes gangrenous and will burst; it also causes a complete obstruction in the intestinal passage, which distends behind the blockage.

I gave the patient 15 milligrams of morphia to ease his pain in the hope that I could reduce the swelling by squeezing it gently back into the abdomen with my fingers, but this was unsuccessful.

Now what was I to do? We were two weeks away from the hospital at Pokhara across an 18,000-foot (5,500-metre) pass to the south and a day from the nearest village. I had half a dozen instruments in a small case I carried solely for sewing up cuts, and a few drugs and dressings in my medicine box. My experience was limited, having been only eighteen months out of medical school, and I had no one to discuss the problem with in order to gain some much-needed moral courage. I had four hill boys as assistants, none of whom had even smelt the inside of a hospital.

One fact was certain: if the obstruction was not relieved he would soon die. I explained this to the relatives and said that if they wished I would operate. The family conferred, huddling together over the body of the sick man, who was allowed little say in his destiny. After much vociferous discussion they told me I should proceed with the operation.

I asked Lakpa to assist me and we set about preparing the patient and organizing our makeshift operating theatre. We put the lama's saddle rugs on the floor of the tent and laid the man in the centre wrapped in a sheepskin coat. The lama had left us and from the adjoining tent came the chant of Buddhist mantras accompanied by the beating of drums, the clash of cymbals and the wail of ceremonial horns. This cacophony set the tone of the proceedings.

We took stock of our tools: one knife, a pair of dissecting forceps, a syringe, a needle holder and three artery clamps, the jaws of which did not meet properly. These were put in a large cooking pot and boiled on a fire outside by one of the Tibetan women. The rest of my instruments were with Sarah across the mountain range.

I gave the patient another two injections of morphia at half-hourly intervals, some phenobarbitone and a pint mug of rakshi, the locally brewed spirit. He slept peacefully. I mustered my helpers and instructed each in the role he had to play. Lakpa, a first-class cook, was my surgical assistant. Babu, who had shown great skill in beheading a ram with one stroke of a kukri at our camp below Hiunchuli Patan, was to do the job of the operating room "scrub" nurse. Dakya, an enormously strong boy who hated the sight of blood, would hold the patient's head, while Sahila stood guard to keep out the howling relatives and inquisitive children.

Lakpa, Babu and I washed our hands thoroughly and packed soap under our nails. Instead of sterile towels for draping the patient, I had some compressed gauze rolls bought in an army surplus store at home. The packets had not been opened and looked fairly clean despite their age. I also had an unopened packet of sterile cotton wool to use for swabs.

We gave the patient some local anaesthetic round the swelling, which was hard and still unreduceable. As we were ready to start I saw a flea hopping across the site prepared for the operation. Lakpa chased it off and nipped it with some forceps. I said a sincere prayer while Babu invoked Hari Krishna from the foot end and Dakya was murmuring "*Om mane padme hum*" at the head. Quite a volume of prayer from three different religions rose through the hole in the roof of the tent where we could see puffs of cumulus scudding across the blue sky above.

I proceeded with great caution, tying off each bleeding point with the cotton Sarah had left me for sewing on my buttons. Lakpa quickly learnt to show me the points of the instruments round which to tie the knots, and Babu's no-touch technique only lapsed once, when he wiped his nose with the back of his hand. Immediately we opened the muscle over the rupture we caught sight of the bowel before it slid back into the abdomen; it did not appear to have become gangrenous. I remembered reading in the textbooks that if forced to do an emergency hernia you should close up as soon as it was reduced and do a formal repair at a later date. However, the man had a five-year history of this trouble and I knew he would never go to hospital for a second operation; if he obstructed again it would be for the last time. So although the area was rather swollen I made the best repair I could with some cotton and closed the wound. The man awoke and grunted disapprovingly as the last stitch went in. Within half an hour a thunderous report from under the blankets told us the obstruction was relieved.

Two hours on my knees bending over the patient had made my back stiff and with relief I stood up outside the tent in the sunlight. Time had flown and it was now late afternoon. The lama's chanting had not ceased all day; I went into his tent and sat sipping Tibetan butter tea in the peace-ful atmosphere, watching butter lamps flicker on the altar.

By evening the patient said he felt, and indeed he looked, much improved, though he was most indignant that I had made his groin so sore. I gave him an injection of penicillin and went to my own tent to sleep.

Next morning I had to move on in order to cross the 18,000-foot (5,500-metre) Mu La before it became impassable with winter snow. Before I left the lama presented me with a white ceremonial scarf in gratitude. I gave instructions and some drugs to the patient's relatives and left at speed.

BUT CONDITIONS at Everest Base Camp hospital were very different now and we felt ready, though not anxious, to undertake any surgery that should be necessary.

CHAPTER 4

Expedition life was a new experience for me, and one that sometimes grated on me during the march-in. This excerpt from a letter tells my feelings about it.

4th of March. Breakfast halt so why don't I tell you about a day of "expedition" life, in the rugged high Himalayas (only really tough guys could manage it).

6:00 a.m. Wakey wakey! — whistle blows. If we had a bugle and someone to blow it no doubt we would have "pukka" reveille. I am in a tent on my own — a privileged position as doctor that I cherish as I can plug in my tape recorder earpiece in the night when I wake up, and go off to sleep again to the peace of a Rossini overture. There is quite a scramble to pack as the Sherpas want to get the loads made up and the coolies sent off, while still providing for the sahibs — how I hate this term but I guess it's there to stick as part of expedition lore.

Breakfast is laid out on tables — all sorts of goodies — tea or coffee, porridge, sugar in abundance and a pile of sweets, fruit bars, figs, chewing gum and candy to help the sahibs manage until the lunch halt. We stroll out of camp leaving the Sherpas to fix the coolie loads, to pack up the tents, put our sleeping bags and mattresses in seabags and clear up the litter about camp.

We walk for three hours till about 10 a.m. So far we have had the usual up and down; steep climbs and long descents that encourage every unused muscle in your legs to raise its voice in protest at ill usage. Since the first day, apart from a brief and spectacular view of Gauri Shankar, we have been out of sight of the snows but all the joy of moving through this beautiful country, sculptured by man from valley floor to hilltop with uncounted terraces, is as tangible as it was when you and I first walked together down the Andhi Khola to Tansen.

Inevitably competition in speed is present in a party of this size. Dougal Haston usually sets off early and gets out in front with a cracking pace. I tried to catch him up the other day and kept pretty close on his heels, but he is immensely fit as he has been skiing all winter and I cannot really tail him at the moment. Maybe in another couple of weeks I will. Carlo usually starts early; since he broke his leg in a skiing accident he walks with a ski stick and has a little trouble going downhill. Michel Vaucher and I go much the same pace. But there is a pleasant change around of companions and always a train of coolies to be overtaken at suitable bends. Many of them have become patients and we exchange cheerful greetings.

A lunch place has been prepared ahead of us by Danu and his kitchen boys and as the wilting sahibs arrive a cup of steaming tea and a platter of fried eggs are thrust into their hands. Ryvita and pumpernickel with butter, raspberry jam or marmalade, Camembert cheese and mayonnaise supplement this meagre fare. We rest a while, write a little and then take off for the afternoon stage.

On arrival at camp in the evening the tents go up, as if by magic, as the sahibs sit round camp tables on aluminium chairs of varying shades and floral patterns to imbibe tea and eat goodies.

I do a clinic when the medical boxes arrive.

Supper by gaslight. Dehydrated soup, dehydrated potatoes, dehydrated vegetable, tinned meat — nothing fresh, no rice, no dal, no tarkari. It is a crazy diet to my way of thinking and I feel sure is contributing to the stomach troubles people are having. I think the sweets and goodies are all very well for later but are hardly necessary now — and a can of beer each day is a luxury

*that can hardly be justified. We have 1200 cans of beer and one porter-load
lasts two days. Fruit juice goes quickly too. When I think of the scrimping and
thought I put into choosing the medical stuff so that it should not be too heavy,
and I find that I have a total of 10 loads — one hundredth part of the total.
If I had known I would have certainly been more liberal — but at least I know
where everything is kept — too much stuff is hard to find your way around.*

*Then we chat for a while and retire to bed while the laughs of the Sherpas
and coolies, well oiled on local spirit, resound over the camp site.*

The march-in was also a time for getting fit, making friendships and for
the expedition members to shake down into a team.

At Thyangboche Naomi Uemura bought a dog. Chomolungma, as it
was called, was a fluffy little Tibetan mastiff mongrel, charming as all
puppies are, and soon Yvette became its adopted mother. Unfortunately
it got off to a bad start by falling into the Sherpas' latrine, from where it
was rescued by Naomi, who gave it a much-needed shampoo.

A problem arose over sexing the animal and Dave Peterson and I
were consulted. He claimed it was a girl. I inspected the nether parts of
the fat, furry underbelly and decided it was a boy. But Dave, who had some
experience of breeding dogs, was right. As I have a diploma in obstetrics
and gynaecology, the others did not think much of my diagnostic acumen
in the field of veterinary science.

Chomo lived in the top of Naomi's rucksack or else stuffed in the
front of his down jacket, and she became a much-loved mascot and grew
fat on the pickings of our table. But like all enchanting babies her attraction waned as she grew into a yapping, snapping little dog. Still Yvette
lavished her attention on Chomo, who slept in the Vauchers' tent at night.

Naomi and his friend Reizo Ito had been to Everest with the Japanese
expedition the year before and had climbed to 26,400 feet (8,000 metres)
in a reconnaissance of the Southwest Face in 1969. Naomi holds the dis-
tinction of having climbed the highest peaks of five continents — Everest
itself in 1970, Mount Kilimanjaro, Mount McKinley, Aconcagua and Mont
Blanc. He is short and strongly built, impeccably polite and friendly,

yet totally unassuming even though, as Reizo told me on the side, "In Japan he berry famos." These were among the very few words of English I ever heard Reizo put together during the expedition. He just smiled and looked too young to be in a party of men.

In the winter before the expedition, Naomi had gone to the Alps with another Japanese climber who had been originally chosen for the team. In a circular letter from Norman Dyhrenfurth we were told, "Konichi has spent twelve days on the Walker Spur of the Jorasses and is in Chamonix Hospital with frostbite. He will have to be replaced." So Reizo Ito took his place.

Seeing these two boyish figures it was difficult to imagine the feats of endurance they had accomplished in the high mountains, or foresee the incredible performance they were going to put up in the months ahead.

One day at our camp at Pheriche, beyond Thyangboche, I was sitting around outside my tent contemplating some exercise to help me acclimatize when the gaunt figure of Dougal Haston lolloped over, his hands stuffed deep in his pockets.

"Are you for a climb today?" he asked casually in his mellow Scots voice. "Yesterday I had a look at the gully yonder and would have soloed it but I didn't have any gear with me."

"Sure, Dougal, but you know I'm not that hot a climber," I replied. "If you're prepared to have me as your second I'm keen to go."

I had done a few gully climbs in Scotland second to Tom Patey and I didn't see why I should not have a go at this one, although I had done no difficult ice climbing for some time and I had never considered myself a master of the craft.

I had begun to know Dougal a little during the preceding weeks so I was very pleased with this unusual sign of friendship. Even though he might not have set off first on the day's march, Dougal would forge ahead, overtaking long lines of coolies on wide bends, and he invariably arrived first at the breakfast halt, where he would be found lazing under a tree reading Tolkien's *Lord of the Rings*. He flatly denied his competitiveness but I only had to be on his heels for a short while before I could feel the pace quicken and he would accelerate into the distance, burning me off like a racing car. In the early days I found I could not trail him but latterly I was getting fit and was well into the swing of walking. I found I could keep up with him as I am a fast walker too and I began to develop an affinity with this reserved and distant character.

So the invitation to join Dougal for this climb was a pleasure, though I had some reservation about volunteering for a day on ice with a climber of his calibre. Dougal was the head of a climbing school at Leysin in Switzerland that advertised with the slogan "Dangle with Dougal." His climbing apprenticeship was served with Edinburgh University, where he was studying for a degree in philosophy. He joined up with a hard, rough school of climbers who were exploring many new routes of extreme difficulty in Scotland, probably the finest all-round mountaineering training ground in the world. All the cliffs are reasonably close to roads, are not too long and offer any standard of rock and ice you care to choose. But within minutes the weather can change and give conditions as vicious as anywhere in the world. Dougal never sat his final exams, the dates of which interfered with his plans to climb the Eiger north face by the direct route. Later he repeated this most difficult of Alpine ascents for the first time ever in winter.

His first visit to the Himalayas was in 1970 when he was in a very strong British team attempting to scale the 7,000-foot (3,800-metre) south face of Annapurna — a complete breakthrough into a new and higher standard of Himalayan climbing. With Don Whillans he reached the summit after a superb team effort.

My seabag with all my climbing equipment had remained at Sete a week back on the march, where all immediately unnecessary loads were left behind when the porters had gone on strike because their leader had absconded after losing 4,000 rupees in a gambling orgy during the night. I borrowed a pair of boots from Norman Dyhrenfurth and some crampons which I adjusted under the critical eye of Don Whillans who, as a professional joiner, was clearly unimpressed with my handling of a screwdriver.

"You'd better stick to t'scalpel, Doc," was his taciturn comment.

Dougal and I crossed the floor of the valley and hopped from boulder to boulder across the river on the far side. A short scramble up steep grass brought us to the foot of the gully, still in deep shadow. Half a mile away we could see the tents of our camp and, removed a couple of hundred yards above it in order to get a full view of the whole gully, Murray Sayle, a journalist on the staff of the *Sunday Times* sent to report the expedition, was sitting in an aluminium chair with his telescope of sixty-times magnification positioned in front of him on a tripod.

We put on the rope and started up the gully, kicking the points of our crampons into the hard ice which gripped with a satisfying crunch. Before long the wall ahead steepened into a large bulge of ice hemmed in on both sides by high vertical walls of rock, with no way of turning the pitch on easy ground. The only way was straight up and over the bulge. I tied myself on to a firm belay of rock and took Dougal's rope round my waist to protect him as he moved out onto the pitch.

Face to face with steep ice, holding a short axe in his hand, Dougal became suddenly transformed; I could see the lean, awkward man with haunted, deep-set eyes, long hair combed forward and hanging over his forehead and ears, prominent jaw and rounded shoulders as the maestro of the Eiger north face, a man who dances on ice with the grace and ease of a mountain goat.

Ice chips flew as he cut steps over the ice bulge, moving up rhythmically and slamming the pointed pick of his axe into the ice ahead to provide a lever to pull on. He rarely bothered to cut steps except at the steepest places, and that was more for me than himself. He adopted the Scottish technique of having a short-handled axe in one hand and a hammer with a pick in the other, and using the points of his crampons he ran up the ice with great agility, not stopping long enough for a step or hold to break away.

The view from the depths of our chasm across the sun-drenched valley to Pokalde, the mountain that I had climbed two years before, was beautiful. I felt deeply content. Dougal at work was totally absorbed, at one with his environment and suddenly relaxed and human in a way I had never seen him before, even when I thought I was getting closer to him. That day I felt a tenuous bond of friendship develop between us and I valued it.

The climb was continuously steep for 1,500 feet (460 metres) and then the gully opened out a little and scattered rocks filled the ravine. We took off our rope and moved quickly over the rough ground, but we soon hit ice again. Dougal went off on his own and found himself unroped out ahead on a very steep section that caused him little apparent concern. I was glad that he threw the rope down for me because, though I found no great difficulty climbing in the steps he had cut, the place was very exposed and a slip would have been fatal.

We were both pleased that the altitude had affected us so little and sat at the top at an altitude of 17,000 feet (5,200 metres) after five hours' steady climbing. We ate some biscuits, drank cold tea and revelled in the delight of a pleasant day's climbing. Dougal normally never says much but then he became quite chatty and his reserve broke for a moment. We crossed a frozen lake and a small neck of land and raced down the hillside back to camp. As we approached, John Evans came out to meet us, carrying a Thermos of hot soup, having followed our progress through binoculars.

Back at camp many of the fellows seemed surprised that the doc was capable of following the maestro up an unclimbed ice gully. "Eh, what's all this pioneering you been at, son?" said Don Whillans. Don in contrast to Dougal was taking his training less strenuously. "That's where I do my acclimatizing," he said, waving at his sleeping bag.

By their achievement on Annapurna, Don Whillans and Dougal Haston proved themselves one of the most formidable climbing pairs in the world. Their diversity of character is probably the foundation of their success and a more unlikely combination is difficult to imagine.

Don is only 37 years old but has adopted the father-figure image of the pair: Dougal is 29. Don has become a legend in the mountaineering world since he began climbing in Wales with Joe Brown when together they created a new standard of rock climbing not only in Britain but in the Alps. At the same time they broke through the class barrier, taking mountaineering away from the exclusiveness of the Alpine Club and the big universities; the hard boys of the Rock and Ice Club, centred round the North, were becoming the top climbers.

Don has mellowed over the years and early pugnacity has given way to an avuncular air, but his Mancunian bluntness remains a frightening barrier to those who do not know him or who may have good reason to fear his penetrating witticisms.

In one of the early team letters, regularly sent out before leaving Europe, Norman Dyhrenfurth suggested that we should each take a short course in one other major language. "What for?" said Don. "I'm climbing with Dougal!"

Don had more experience of the Himalayas than anyone else on the expedition except the leaders; in fact, for more than half the members this was their first visit. He has been on expeditions to Masherbrum and Trivor in the Karakoram, and to Gauri Shankar and Annapurna. He went to Huandoy in the Patagonian Andes and has climbed widely in North America. His Alpine record, too, was as extensive as those climbers whose home ground was in the Alps.

So, on experience, Don was a strong contender for the leadership of the Face team. Whether his tact would allow him to keep a party of such diverse people happy was uncertain. His sense of humour was quite unintelligible to the Americans and the continentals and his casual attitude to the expedition was a constant mystery. He arrived nearly a month after the main party in appalling physical condition with a beer-drinker's paunch that overflowed the tops of his trousers, the top button of which he was unable to fasten. After the first half day of walking he was nursing his blisters and coughing away the emanations of the pungent little cigars that he smoked continually. His pace, when he could not avoid walking, was very slow and on arrival in camp he would sit for hours outside his tent doing nothing but contemplate.

"How can this be the famous Don Whillans?" others asked, wagging their heads sadly after one glance at the man backed by the press to climb Everest. "He won't go high."

"Shouldn't overdo the training, son," Don would say, "They'll burn 'emselves out early, they will." Such was the confidence of a man who knows his own capabilities. This casualness could be irritating and many people resented the fact that Don and Dougal had taken no part in the hard work of preparing for the expedition and showed little inclination to make up for it by offering themselves to help with the many jobs that needed doing on-site. But Norman Dyhrenfurth was prepared to overlook these idiosyncrasies in expectation of the contribution they might make on the mountain.

DON, DOUGAL, Murray Sayle and I went down for a drink to the inn at the end of Pheriche village.

As I was leaving the chhang house I bumped into a very broad and strong Tibetan porter with whom I had made friends, Tobgyel Bhotia by name. His long hair was plaited with pink ribbon and tied over his forehead. When he smiled, as he did most of the time, his wide mouth showed two rows of big teeth, several of which were made of gold. He spoke with a throaty roar that boomed deeper and louder the more drunk he became, and he was in the habit of knocking his head against that of his neighbour over a glass of chhang as a sign of friendship; but when inebriated he was unaware of his own strength and these blows could knock one silly.

We drank another glass together, tested the strength of our grip across the bar table and left him, then walked back to camp in the dark. Murray became garrulous.

"I rather fancied this assignment," he said in his rough Australian drawl, a toothpick hanging from the corner of his mouth. "See, I sailed across the Atlantic in a small boat myself so I was sent to cover [Francis] Chichester rounding the Horn. I'd been following his progress closely for a week or two and was getting pushed to get my piece in. So I sat down with my typewriter in a hotel in Buenos Aires with half a bottle of gin and bashed out the story of his rounding Cape Horn in one night flat. Must say I ran a bit thin on the nautical terms by the time six-foot waves had crashed over his bowsprit and he gybed to windward several paragraphs running." Two weeks later Chichester was located well out into the South Atlantic and Murray was made reporter of the year.

"So I came on this circus as a different way of making bread and guessed I was going to watch the action through my telescope from a safe distance sipping pineapple juice cocktails." After Murray had seen Norman Dyhrenfurth's film *Americans on Everest* in Kathmandu, he was a little shattered to realize he would not see any action from Base Camp and would have to go up through the Icefall to get his stories.

None of us could really fathom Murray. Physically he must have been the most unathletic-looking man ever to have approached the slopes of Everest. He is tall with drooping, rounded shoulders and a belly that could only just be contained by his leather belt; his nose is beaked and pointed at the tip and his jowls are flabby and covered with greying stubble. He is a hard, outback Australian who in the rough, tough, no-holds-barred world of journalism has risen to the top of his profession.

Soon after he disembarked from the boat taking him to Britain from Australia, where he was born, he got a job with *The People*. His serial "How I took a lorry ride to shame" ran on for seventeen consecutive weeks and launched him into British journalism. He went off to report the Soviet invasion of Czechoslovakia still wearing his Atlantic yachting cap with the salt water barely dry on his canvas shoes, and he returned in a baggy, middle-European suit and cloth cap. After the Six Day War in the Middle East he wandered round the corridors of the office in Israeli combat gear; he visited Castro in Cuba, and in Bolivia he made a scoop by discovering Che Guevara's guerrilla hideout; recently he had spent two years reporting the war in Vietnam. At an age when most active journalists have taken to their desks he is still tasting every exciting experience possible, yet this was his first time on a mountain.

I was astonished to discover that the expedition was going to be reported so closely and expressed my concern to a friend. "I wouldn't speak to Murray Sayle till it's all over and you're back in Kathmandu," was his advice. But I am glad I didn't take it, as Murray became a good friend.

In Kathmandu he hired a bicycle and, wearing a tartan deerstalker, short trousers and a T-shirt with "Bloomsbury Wheelers" emblazoned across his chest, pedalled round the city honking a klaxon he bought in the market at all the sacred cows lying in the roadway.

On the approach march he changed his dress to that of a field combat soldier from the jungles of Vietnam; jungle-green battle jacket, floppy jungle hat, regulation water bottle and dull green trousers with huge pockets stuffed with camera gear.

I got to know Murray better on the march-in, especially after Thyangboche, when he became more and more concerned about his health. He had gone fairly slowly till then but he rarely complained as he staggered into camp long after everyone else nursing some aching muscle or painful blister.

Snow had fallen at Thyangboche and the path was very slippery by the time a hundred yaks had gone before and churned up the icy mud. Murray had acquired a large staff like a small tree trunk that he used to steady himself and we set off together through the rhododendron woods before the sun had broken through. He refused to take any advice and alternately slithered down the steeper sections of the path on the seat of his pants or sidestepped onto the bank to avoid getting the horn of a passing yak up his backside.

"How'm I doin', Doc?" he asked frequently.

"Fine, Basa, keep it up," I replied, subduing my impatience as we advanced at the pace of a snail.

Uphill he went better, but progress was dreadfully slow and he became increasingly health-conscious as we rose. Above Pangboche, passing the graves of two trekkers who had died of high-altitude edema within the past three years, Murray was thrown into a fit of acute hypochondria, so I had to take his pulse and give him firm reassurance.

I was amazed at the way he prepared his "piece" for the *Sunday Times*. It had to be finished for the mail runner to reach Lukla on Friday to catch the plane to Kathmandu, from where it would go to New Delhi and arrive by Saturday morning in London. Most of the week Murray would lie in his tent in a morass of untidy confusion, reading one of the seven volumes of Gibbon's *Decline and Fall of the Roman Empire* that he had brought to pass the time. Occasionally he would foray from his tent for a call to the latrine or a meal and would repeat his question, "How'm I doin', Doc?" I began to fear I would have to treat him for bedsores before he was finished. On the evening before the mail runner's departure he would amble around camp wearing his voluminous blue duck-down drawers and waistcoat, chewing hard on a toothpick and murmuring, "D'you think I ought to cobble up some prose for tomorrow?"

Despite urgent encouragement he would do nothing until everyone had gone to bed and then the tapping of the typewriter could be heard from the mess tent. Murray would sit crouched in the light of a paraffin lamp, his feet on a hot water bottle ("to warm up my brain"), knocking words together to send off to "the abrasive-tongued meritocrats" who were sitting behind their desks in Bloomsbury.

CHAPTER 5

"The harm comes from the quality of the air one breathes in and out since it is so extremely thin and delicate," wrote Fra Joseph da Costa in 1608 about the high mountains of the South American Andes. The thinness of the air he described affects mountaineers at altitude in all parts of the world. I will try to explain how the mountaineer is affected in language someone who is not a specialist can follow, and so I hope to enable the reader to understand some of the problems we met on Everest.

The air we breathe at sea level is composed of four parts nitrogen and one part oxygen, and although this ratio does not change with increasing altitude, the density or quantity of these gases becomes less. As the atmospheric pressure falls with increasing altitude, so the pressure exerted by its constituent gases, oxygen and nitrogen, also diminishes; so that at 18,000 feet (5,500 metres) — Base Camp — the oxygen pressure is half of that at sea level and on the summit of Everest at 29,028 feet (8,848 metres) it is less than one third. An ordinary weather barometer can, for this reason, be used as an altimeter. The higher one climbs the thinner the air becomes, and life would not be possible if the body did not make adjustments to compensate for the lack of pressure to force oxygen into the tissues, especially those of the brain. A pressure is needed to force the oxygen across the delicate membranes in the lungs into the blood, where the red cells carry it to distant parts of the body, in the same way as a firefighter requires not only large amounts of water but also a pump to deliver it at high pressure. Oxygen is released to the tissues and becomes the essential fuel for the normal function of every type of cell; when it is burnt up by cell metabolism it forms a waste product, carbon dioxide, which is breathed to the outside air.

As the mountaineer climbs higher and higher, so the air he breathes contains oxygen at lower and lower pressure and the time will come when this pressure is no longer adequate to force oxygen in sufficient quantities to the tissues; if the brain is totally deprived for more than a few minutes the person dies rapidly.

Climbers who are short of oxygen for long periods of time could theoretically suffer from brain damage. But all the four men who went to 28,000 feet (8,500 metres) on Everest in 1933 subsequently had distinguished careers. A recent television interview with three octogenarian Everesters, Odell, Somervell and Noel, only serves to advertise the healthy life in the cold thin air up high.

The first signs of oxygen lack occur at about 5,000 feet (1,500 metres) and with increasing altitude the thinness of the air causes troublesome headaches, difficulty in sleeping and a nasal quality in the speech. Because of the diminished air resistance it gives some advantage to sprinters and short-distance runners, as was shown in the Olympic Games held at Mexico City (2,254 metres) in 1968. If the body made no adjustments life would be insupportable above 7,000 feet (2,100 metres); acclimatization is the process by which the body learns to cope with the situation of living under diminished oxygen pressure.

The first known facts about acclimatization were learnt in the South American Andes. The Incas of Peru in the sixteenth century had laws which prevented slaves being moved from the sea coast up to sulphur mines in the mountains and working alongside men who had lived all their lives at these altitudes and were naturally acclimatized.

Aucanquilcha, the highest sulphur mine in Chile, lies at 19,000 feet (5,800 metres) and the present-day Indians who work there prefer to live in quarters at 17,500 feet (5,300 metres) and travel up and down daily, which suggests that the critical height for permanent acclimatization is around 18,000 feet (5,500 metres). The speed of acclimatization varies between mountaineers and may explain why some are able to tolerate very high altitudes. In the eighteenth century scientists did not believe that man could stay alive on the high peaks of the Alps, yet in 1786 the village doctor from Chamonix, Michel Gabriel Paccard, as a result of a challenge from Monsieur H. B. de Saussure, climbed to the summit of Mont Blanc and returned fit and well to tell the tale.

On Mount Everest in 1924 Noel Odell spent eleven nights consecutively at over 23,000 feet (7,000 metres) without oxygen, while searching for the missing climbers George Mallory and Andrew Irvine. During this time he climbed six times up and down between Camp III (21,000 feet, 6,400 metres) and Camp IV (23,000 feet, 7,000 metres), once from the North Col to Camp V (25,500 feet, 7,800 metres) and twice within four days to 27,000 feet (8,200 metres). Of this unprecedented feat Odell said, "Our evidence has shown us emphatically that one can live and feel fit for an indefinite period at 23,000 feet [7,000 metres] ... there seems no reason at all to suppose that this important physiological capability, acclimatization, other things being equal, should not be possible at an altitude equivalent to that of the top of Mount Everest." But Odell had extraordinary physique and was described by Norton, deputy leader of the expedition, as "a climber of unequalled endurance and toughness." In 1933 Frank Smythe spent three nights at 27,400 feet (8,350 metres) without oxygen. More than twenty ascents to 28,000 feet (8,500 metres) without the use of additional oxygen are now recorded.

In 1875 Tissandier and two colleagues ascended to 29,000 feet (8,800 metres) in a balloon and two of them died. Part of the explanation for these contrasting experiences lies in the speed of ascent to altitude. In the early Everest expeditions the route through Tibet was long and involved, crossing several high passes, so acclimatization was well under way by the time the climbers were at risk. Because balloonists and aircraft pilots reach high altitude before acclimatization has started they must use oxygen above 10,000 feet (3,000 metres), not only to survive but to be able to fly their machines safely.

The physiological process of acclimatization is central to the whole question of high-altitude mountaineering. Oxygen is essential for the life and function of all cells in the body and the more sensitive the cell the greater is its demand for oxygen. If deprived of oxygen the brain cells will die in less than four minutes while the heart, the cells of which are not so delicate, may go on beating for much longer. All the physiological processes in acclimatization are ultimately directed to one end: to keep the body adequately supplied with oxygen. The first and rapid phase of acclimatization starts at about 5,000 feet (1,500 metres). The reduction of oxygen pressure in the atmosphere, in the lungs and in the blood, is first detected by small receptor organs located in the main arteries to the brain. These receptors cause the respiratory centres in the brain to be stimulated and as a result the depth and frequency of breathing increase, which may be the first thing the mountaineer notices. With deeper breathing, carbon dioxide, which dilutes oxygen in the lungs, is removed more rapidly and its concentration in the blood is reduced. Although the pressure of oxygen in the atmosphere falls, the effect is mitigated by the lowering of carbon dioxide so that oxygen pressure in blood and tissues does not fall so greatly.

Breathing not only becomes deep but also irregular at altitude and takes the form of periodic, or Cheyne-Stokes, respiration. The pattern consists of a gradual increase in the depth of breathing which rises to a peak, then declines slowly and ceases for a few seconds before the cycle is repeated. The phenomenon is experienced by everyone arriving at altitude: it is most common at night and gives rise to some anxiety — particularly during the short periods when respiration ceases. The cause of this type of respiration is unknown. It is commonly seen in newborn babies shortly after birth — for whom, of course, breathing is a new experience — and invariably in babies born at altitude, for example in families of lead miners in the American Rockies at 11,000 feet (3,300 metres). Although precipitated by a lack of oxygen, it probably represents an unstable response to the changes in carbon dioxide caused by the persistently raised level in respiration. In both babies and mountaineers this type of respiration passes off in hours or days as respiration becomes set at a new level.

Stimulation of the oxygen receptors also causes two other important effects. At about 18,000 feet (5,500 metres) there is a clear increase in the speed and force of the heart's contraction, which the climber senses as palpitations. As a consequence the volume of blood circulating each minute increases and, as no extra oxygen is extracted with each circulation, the pressure of oxygen in the tissues is higher than it would have been. In addition, the low oxygen causes an increase in the rate of production of red blood cells which may take four to six weeks to complete. At altitude blood can carry up to a third more oxygen than at sea level but unfortunately at the same time it becomes thicker and more viscous.

The blood is made even thicker because the volume of plasma, which suspends the red cells, decreases due to the lack of oxygen stimulating the sympathetic nerves to constrict the walls of the veins and so eliminate the normal pool of blood in the periphery of the body.

The consequence of this abnormal stickiness of the blood is twofold. The heart is put under more strain by the increased work required to pump the thick blood through it, and there is more danger of small vessels forming clots which cause blockages or thromboses. In 1933 on Everest Eric Shipton lost his speech for a short while, presumably due to a small stroke affecting the speech centre in his brain. Edmund Hillary had a more severe but temporary stroke climbing Makalu in 1960.

The thickness of the blood may be further accentuated by loss of body water with dehydration. Heavy breathing in the cold, dry atmosphere on the high mountains, together with sweating due to heavy work wearing insulated clothes, causes the loss of much body water. Between five and seven litres of fluid per day should be drunk at altitudes over 20,000 feet (6,100 metres).

All these points indicate that the various parts of the acclimatization process start at different altitude levels and proceed at different rates. Some people are never troubled by altitude provided they ascend slowly enough, while others, for no obvious physical reason, can never acclimatize properly however long they remain high. This feature of altitude is very individual and idiosyncratic. Ironically, acclimatization is not a continuing process. Deterioration starts after about one month at high altitude, but this time varies markedly with different people. The climber's capacity for work falls off and he suffers from poor appetite and loss of weight and he cannot sleep properly. He may also experience hallucinations, as Smythe did in 1933 when he was descending alone to Camp VI. He was so convinced that he was roped to some invisible companion that he turned and offered the mythical figure half his Kendal Mint-Cake; he also saw two hovering, pulsating kite balloons in the sky. If the mountaineer is going to be able to reach altitudes of more than 20,000 feet (6,100 metres) and also to perform the hard work of climbing and carrying loads, the lower part of the climb should be as leisurely as possible. It is also probable that acclimatization alone cannot sustain life and heavy work at high altitude, and oxygen may have to be added from cylinders carried on the back. This is a problem which has been debated with intensity ever since the first attempts to climb Everest.

In 1922, when the oxygen cylinders were heavy, bulky and cumbersome, Mallory wrote, "For my part, I don't think it impossible to get up without oxygen ... nothing in the experience of the first attempt has led me to suppose that those last 2,000 feet [600 metres] cannot be climbed in a day."

Dr. T. Howard Somervell wrote of the 1922 expedition:

It seems that the chances of climbing the mountain are probably greater if oxygen be not used. For ... in an attempt without oxygen only three or four coolies are required for the camping equipment and the food at the highest camp. It were better to prepare for a number of attempts each by a small but acclimatized party rather than to stake all on one or two highly organized endeavours, in which oxygen, and a large number of coolies are used.

Norton, in 1924, said, "I still believe that there is nothing in the atmospheric conditions even between 28,000 and 29,000 feet (8,500 and 8,800 metres) to prevent a fresh and fit party from reaching the top without oxygen." Odell reported his own experience at about 26,000 feet (7,900 metres) thus: "Oxygen gave so little effect and the apparatus proved such an irksome load that I was glad to hand the outfit over to a porter to carry ..." and again, "On my second ascent to that altitude (27,000 feet, 8,200 metres) I used oxygen from Camp V at 25,000 feet (7,600 metres) but at rather over 26,000 feet (7,900 metres) I felt I was deriving so little benefit from it that I turned it off and did not use the gas again ... I felt able to progress altogether better than when I had been breathing oxygen ... without the bulk and awkwardness of the apparatus."

Rutledge summarizes the experiences of the 1933 expedition thus, "... a climber will receive little or no benefit from the use of oxygen at an altitude to which he has acclimatized himself in the natural way." And Raymond Greene, the doctor on the party, said, "The condition of the climbers at 28,000 feet (8,500 metres) was so good that there is little doubt of their capacity, in good condition, to climb Everest without oxygen."

But George Finch, the designer of the oxygen system in 1922 and its greatest exponent, was still adamant many years after. "The climbing of Mount Everest is ... very close to the limit of human endeavour. As such it calls for the exercise of every advantage that the wit of man can devise." Tilman in 1938 reverts to the common view, "I am not convinced on this year's showing that the advantages conferred by using oxygen outweigh the ethical objections to its use."

No one has yet climbed Everest without oxygen. However, Edmund Hillary was able to do enough mental arithmetic on the final part of the climb to work out how much oxygen he had left in his cylinders and when he reached the summit he removed his mask for ten minutes and took many excellent photographs. In 1963 four men, Willi Unsoeld, Tom Hornbein, Barry Bishop and Lute Jerstad, were forced to bivouac in the open air above 28,000 feet (8,500 metres) on the way down from the summit of Everest. Their oxygen had run out and although frostbitten they survived the night, which, by a miracle, was windless. Don Whillans and Dougal Haston on their ascent of the south face of Annapurna were doing difficult alpine-standard climbing up to 26,000 feet (7,900 metres), only using oxygen for sleeping.

The foregoing paragraphs give the views and experiences of some of the great men of Everest. On our expedition three hundred bottles of oxygen were brought to the mountain under the supervision of Dr. Duane Blume, a high-altitude physiologist at the White Mountain Research Station perched on top of a peak in the Sierras of California. Before the expedition he had little more experience of mountains than the twice weekly helicopter flight up to the airy landing pad of his laboratory, and a week's crash instruction course in climbing.

Duane is a kindly man with a genial smile and the slow, drawling accent I associate with the traditional cinema cowboy. Lean and spare in build, he appeared more suited to his domestic role of a devoted father of eight children. By his very detachment from the intensity of the tough professional mountaineers he was able to add a measure of sanity and moderation to the expedition. Duane was largely responsible for the design of the oxygen system, which took him a large part of the previous year. It was an improvement on the Hornbein system used with success by the Americans in 1963.

The oxygen content should be the same for each breath regardless of the rate of breathing. Thus for men doing a short burst of hard work, who might double their normal number of breaths per minute, the supply would adjust to keep pace with the demand. The tanks held 1,180 litres of oxygen at a pressure of 3,000 pounds per square inch (211 kilograms per square centimetre) and when full weighed a little over sixteen pounds (seven kilograms). Attached to the cylinder was an on/off valve that reduced the pressure in the tank to sixty pounds p.s.i. (four kilograms p.s.c.) before it entered the tubing; without this reducing valve, the pressure coming direct from the tank would be far too high.

A novel feature — the real clockwork of the system — was a neat little diluter-demand regulator unit the size of a fist, which was attached to the oxygen cylinder by polyurethane tubing and worn strung round the neck. A dial, with four settings that could easily be changed by hand, adjusted the mixing of outside atmospheric air with oxygen from the tank to dilute the oxygen concentration in the inspired air to an equivalent height of 17,500 feet (5,300 metres). Dial number 1 was used up to 25,000 feet (7,600 metres), dial 2 to 27,000 feet (8,200 metres), dial 3 to 29,000 feet (8,800 metres) and dial 4 above that or if a high concentration of oxygen was required for a particular effort of work. The system, like all clever inventions, was simple in design and easy to understand.

Corrugated rubber tubing connected the diluter-demand valve by a simple fitting to the rubber face mask of standard U.S. Air Force design. Made of rubber, it could easily be crushed in the hand to break up any ice that formed by moisture freezing on the outlet valve. The mask was clipped onto a cloth helmet by two simple wire catches lying over the cheeks.

The Blume system is an open circuit apparatus; the person breathes a mixture of air and added oxygen and exhales to the atmosphere outside. In a closed circuit system, as used by Charles Evans and Tom Bourdillon on Everest in 1953, the person inhales a high concentration of oxygen from a breathing bag and exhales through a canister of soda lime, which absorbs the carbon dioxide produced in the lungs. The exhaled gas returns to the breathing bag and is used again many times. In theory this system is ideal, but the soda lime absorbers are bulky and the apparatus is very hot to wear.

In order to do hard climbing on Everest a reliable system is needed: this one fulfilled the requirements well.

CHAPTER 6

Now that the highest hospital in the world, of which we were inordinately proud, had been built we were ready to start in business. And business descended upon us in an unexpected and dramatic way.

On March 26, three days after we reached Base Camp, a young Spanish climber pitched his tent a hundred yards down the moraine. He came up to Base Camp after breakfast next morning and explained he was from the Alpine Club of Bilbao, which had applied to the Nepal government for permission to attempt to climb Mount Everest in 1974. He was an experienced climber who had been to the Alps several times and to the Caucasus range, as well as doing many hard routes in the Pyrenees, his own home ground and one that I also dearly love. He had been selected to do a reconnaissance on behalf of his club and to gather as much information and expertise as possible.

He passed the morning talking to Norman Dyhrenfurth and Jimmy Roberts; two more experienced men would have been difficult to find, so this was a stroke of luck for him.

I had talked with him little more than to pass the time of day, but he struck me as being pale beside my healthy and now bronzed companions. I went about my business, which that day was devoted to learning from Duane Blume the finer points of the oxygen system he had designed and which I needed to adapt for medical use. I wanted the equipment to be ready at hand in the hospital with two loaded cylinders in case we were suddenly caught with an emergency.

Duane and I were engrossed in our task with valves, spanners and pieces of corrugated rubber piping scattered round the floor of the hospital when Michel Vaucher appeared at the door, followed by the Spaniard walking unsteadily and supported on Yvette's arm.

"He has a bad head and I think he's ill. He has been sitting with us in the tent but I thought I'd bring him over to see you," said Michel with concern.

Duane and I took one glance at the man's waxy, ashen face and dusky lips tinged with mauve, and the same thoughts went through our heads — "Lack of oxygen, blue blood, cyanosis —"

"Thank you, Michel," I said. "We'll take care of him. I think it's best if he stays here. Please could you ask his Sherpa to bring his own things over from their tent?"

The Spaniard sat down on the corner bed and I asked him how he felt, but even with the exertion of speaking his colour became more blue. So we laid him down and Duane fitted a cloth helmet on his head to which an oxygen mask could be clipped and held firmly to his face. By closing off the air entry to the diluter-demand valve with his hand, Duane administered pure oxygen to the patient. The result was striking. After several puffs, pink colouring returned to the patient's cheeks and when we removed the mask his lips had regained their normal redness.

"Let's leave the mask off a while and see what happens," said Duane.

Within a minute the climber's pinkness drained away and he turned a dusky purple hue. I listened to his chest with my stethoscope and could detect the crackling sounds of fluid accumulating in the fine air passages of the normally dry lungs; shortly afterwards he coughed up some blood-flecked sputum and became increasingly breathless. His temperature was normal. I came to the conclusion that he was suffering from acute mountain sickness.

In this condition, also called high-altitude edema, water accumulates in the body tissues for reasons that are not clearly understood. It seems likely that the kidneys are unable to get rid of body fluid as efficiently as usual; maybe the fine capillary blood vessels of the lung become more permeable and leak plasma owing to the lack of oxygen in the thin mountain air. The end result is that accumulated fluid settles in the lungs (pulmonary edema) or in the brain (cerebral edema).

High-altitude pulmonary edema is a condition that has only been described in the past ten years. In mountain literature many unexplained deaths are reported vaguely as "heart strain" or "pneumonia" and it seems likely that several of these were unrecognized eases of pulmonary edema.

It is not possible to determine in advance what sort of person is likely to suffer from the disease. Those who rise to altitude quickly seem more prone, but fully acclimatized persons have succumbed; young and old, fit and unfit, experienced climbers and inexpert trekkers have all appeared in reports of cases from the mountains.

The usual picture is as follows: a healthy person arrives at any altitude above 12,000 feet (3,700 metres) and feels mountain sick because the air is thin and lacking in oxygen. Normal people commonly have unpleasant early symptoms at height, but the patient with acute mountain sickness is more ill than would be expected in the given circumstances. He descends because he feels so wretched and immediately he improves; so he climbs high again, falls ill and may die very quickly before help can be obtained.

This classical course of events happened to Bob Downes, a friend of mine from Cambridge, who died on Masherbrum in the Karakoram range in 1957; it was the first time that high-altitude pulmonary edema was clearly recognized.

Since that time more and more people becoming sick in the mountains have been seen to be suffering from pulmonary edema. In Colorado and in the Peruvian Andes much research work has been done, but the largest number of reported cases is from India. Many Indian troops were flown from the plains to heights of over 11,000 feet (3,300 metres) in Ladakh and Leh in northern Kashmir on the Tibet-India border during their conflict with China in 1962. The Indian military doctors discovered that many of their troops were succumbing to acute mountain sickness; field hospitals being available, they were able to carry out sophisticated investigations into this illness. But even their observations are inconclusive and much needs to be learnt before we fully understand this disease that can attack anyone going into the high mountains and, without speedy recognition and treatment, may be rapidly fatal.

Having made a diagnosis on my patient I sat down and thought about treatment. The Spaniard was lying in the corner of the hospital curled up in his purple sleeping bag, which he closely matched when his mask was off. Crinkled rubber tubing led to the brown and green oxygen cylinders propped on a rock beside his bed. I felt that so long as I could keep him well on oxygen alone I would do so until we could arrange evacuation to a lower altitude, which is the specific remedy for the illness.

Many people have advocated the use of a diuretic drug frusemide (Lasix) that helps people to lose dammed-up water from the body tissues. But I had a frightening experience with this drug when I was at Kunde Hospital in 1969. I was helping Doctor Evans, the New Zealander in charge, to treat a young Swiss nurse who had been carried into the hospital with advanced pulmonary edema bubbling in her chest. We had given her an injection of frusemide into a vein and she suddenly collapsed owing to an adverse reaction to the drug and became so ill she nearly died. So I was wary of using it again until I felt forced to do so. I left Ang Tsering watching the patient and went over to Norman Dyhrenfurth's tent to discuss the problem with him.

"I know he's not our responsibility, Norman," I said, "but nevertheless we can't leave him under a pile of stones on the glacier. And that will surely happen if we don't get him out of here in a hurry."

"Well, Peter, I'll leave the decision to you. We can always call a helicopter from Kathmandu. But he'll have to pay. Has he any money?" asked Norman.

"I don't know but I'll find out," I said. "I guess his alpine club could always pay."

"It's a lot of money at 350 bucks an hour," said Norman.

"I know," I replied, "but it's either that or a pile of stones. How about you coming to have a look at him so I can show you I'm not making a fuss?"

Norman Dyhrenfurth, Jimmy Roberts and Carlo Mauri, who speaks Spanish, came over to the hospital and I was able to demonstrate to them the dramatic change in the Spaniard's colour after removing the mask for a minute. Norman was assured.

"No doubt about it, he's sick, Peter. Sure we'd better send a message first thing in the morning to lift him out of here."

I settled down to a night of watchfulness and Murray Sayle offered to come and sit with me to help pass the hours. The Spaniard was fine while the oxygen was running continuously, so we counted his respiration and pulse rate at intervals, keeping an eye on his colour meanwhile. By coincidence Antony Thomas had a tape recording of a Spanish bullfight with the sounds of olés, and it cheered our patient a little; then we turned the tape over and sedated him with boleros, so that he drifted off to sleep.

Murray Sayle and I got out the chess set and played a couple of games, which I won. He expostulated on my luck and we chatted till long into the night.

About midnight I checked the valve on the oxygen set to see that there was sufficient oxygen in the cylinder to administer an adequate flow to the patient. I found that the needle on the dial had not shifted during the previous hour and, as I had been assured by Duane Blume that a bottle would only last four to six hours, I estimated that this one should be nearly empty. I guessed the needle had jammed.

I knew the Spaniard could last less than a minute without oxygen, so this was a matter of urgency.

"Hang on here and watch him, Basa," I said to Murray, "I'm going over to the oxygen tent to get another valve."

Outside the hospital tent the night was clear and the air crisp with the temperature registering -12°C. A sky full of stars shone in the black vault over Pumori and Lhotse, which looked close and large in the darkness. I felt an intense loneliness surrounded by so many sleeping men in their orange tents on this piece of utterly deserted barren ground.

I ran past the radio tent, down the khud and across a stream on the path towards the tent where the oxygen was stored, well away from camp in case of an explosion. The distance was no more than a hundred yards but exerting myself at this height in the freezing air started a hacking bout of coughing, something that I had been troubled with since an attack of influenza some weeks before. I felt a searing pain in the right side of my chest that was so intense it took my breath away. I collapsed outside the oxygen tent and just pulled myself together enough to crawl inside.

I could not imagine what had happened. I was unable to breathe deeply, could only manage a shallow panting and the pain was like red-hot knives thrust into my side. I sat down on an empty case and after rummaging through the boxes of oxygen equipment I found a complete valve set. I walked slowly back to the hospital and changed the valve and the cylinder.

When I sat still the pain eased so I sent Murray off to bed, grateful for all the help he had given. I woke Ang Tsering and asked him to watch the Spaniard while I lay down on a mattress on the floor beside him. But I had such heavy Cheyne-Stokes breathing that I could not sleep and the pain grew steadily worse.

I took over from Ang Tsering after an hour and a half and went to the kitchen for a while to make a cup of tea on the wood fire in the hope of finding a comfortable position to sit in. The kitchen workers were snoring loudly in their sleeping bags laid out on the stony floor around the fire that had long since died and had provided no warmth after the first two hours of the night.

By 6 a.m. I could only breathe shallowly and it hurt to talk. I crawled over to Murray's tent to ask his advice. Doctors are so used to handing out counsel to other people that I felt peculiarly helpless being on the receiving end for a change. I felt very low, partly because of the pain, partly owing to lack of sleep and the fearsome prospect of something serious having occurred inside my chest. At first I thought I had a spontaneous pneumothorax, which happens when one of the bubble alveoli at the very end of the lung ruptures and lets air into the vacuum normally present around the lung to keep it expanded against the chest cage.

Murray gave the sound, commonsense advice I was seeking and knew I should get from him. "You've got to get out of here, Peter, and have a rest. Might as well go all the way to Kathmandu with this joker, as he's got to go anyway. Then you can see a proper doc and get an x-ray."

I would be able to have a full medical check in Kathmandu. I knew Dr. Selwyn Lang had no x-ray at Kunde and I wanted confirmation that I would be fit to go high on the mountain.

I agreed with Murray, so went to discuss the matter with Norman Dyhrenfurth. I asked him particularly not to tell the rest of the men I was sick, as this was a dangerous time in the Icefall and they needed all the support they could get. Norman was emphatic, "You're going down as his escort and will return immediately. That takes care of it. We'll tell them not to send anyone extra when we radio for the helicopter."

I went to lie in my tent, waiting for the helicopter to come. We estimated it would arrive around midday. Leo Schlömmer, an alpine instructor in the Austrian army who specialized in mountain rescue work, took charge of preparing a landing pad on the glacier for the helicopter. Such an exercise was Leo's bread and butter and he carried it out with appropriate skill. He chose the only flat place in the area, a small frozen lake about forty yards across, surrounded by the pinnacles of the Khumbu glacier and the rubble of the moraine. With the help of the Sherpas he laid out a marker square, cleared a pad free of stones and settled down to wait.

Leo is fair-haired with a shy and youthful look. He was engaged to be married on his return from the expedition and received a steady and profuse stream of mail from the home of his beloved in Innsbruck. "This is my first bivouac," he explained with a wry smile, showing a photo of an attractive blonde sitting on a double bed.

Leo has wide experience as a professional climbing and skiing guide; he has been on expeditions to Jirishanka in Peru and to Momhil Sar in the Karakoram. He has climbed the notorious north face of the Eiger and many of the hard routes in California's Yosemite Valley. Because of his mountain rescue skill Leo was put in charge of the three steel winches brought with a view to installing them on the Face and hauling equipment up to save the man-hauling of loads. In theory it was a very good idea but in practice the steel cable cut deep into the ice and snagged.

Just before midday a faint, high-pitched murmur was heard. It grew steadily louder and soon the helicopter appeared against the face of Pumori flying at about 20,000 feet (6,100 metres). It circled like a huge dragonfly, its sinister buzzing coming closer and closer. After surveying the scene in a long, high, circling movement it dropped and flew low over the prepared pad where Leo was making signs with his arms to indicate the landing site. It returned and hovered some feet above the ground and then settled gently like a predator on its prey. I had meanwhile collected the Spaniard with the help of some Sherpas who carried him four hundred yards across the moraine on one of the toboggan stretchers brought for rescue work.

The French helicopter pilot climbed out of his bubble cockpit, casually dressed in flannel shirt and bell-bottomed jeans, and took a couple of whiffs from his flying oxygen mask. Contrary to our radio instructions he had brought along a "Spanish-speaking doctor," who was obviously a French friend of his who had come for the ride.

I told him I was going to escort the patient to Kathmandu. This caused a problem of weight because of his superfluous friend, who had no specialized knowledge of the patient's condition and had brought no equipment of any use in the circumstances. I was incensed when the pilot said, "C'est pas une promenade pour touristes ceci." I was in too much discomfort to argue and left Jimmy Roberts to sort out the pilot, who reluctantly decided to take one person down the valley and return for the patient on a second trip to lighten the load as, owing to the thin air, the helicopter could not gain height. Carlo Mauri embraced me; I was very touched and assured him I would be back soon. I climbed into the cabin in order not to miss my seat.

The turbo-jet engines broke into life, the blades began to turn and slowly gathered speed. The pilot eased the stick gradually and the tail of the helicopter rose in the air, the nose dipped and we moved forwards, pointing down the glacier. We were soon in Phantom Alley among the ice towers flashing past first on one side then on the other as he wove a course in and out like skiing a slalom.

I was terrified and glanced anxiously at the pilot as the engine gave a strange roar in a burst to gain height to clear the ice. He calmly gave the thumbs-up sign, from which I gained much reassurance. The pinnacles took on more fantastic shapes from the air than from the ground, sculpted to an individual beauty, white and shining sharply, with caverns of ghostly blue excavated from their bases where the stream undercut the bank. Icicles hung like organ pipes but no music sounded from them, just the creaking of the shattered glacier, the tumble of water and now the roar of our engines. The time of danger can only have lasted some seconds, maybe a few minutes even, but the intensity of fear exaggerated the feeling of time.

The phantom spires of the glacier fell away below us as we swung over Gorak Shep and followed the line of moraine rock towards the bar of snow peaks to the south. Turning sharply east, we flew over Pheriche and the pattern of the huts and stone-walled fields was clear down below us. As we turned again into the valley leading down to Thyangboche the pilot clung to the eastern bank, cut his engines and settled down in a potato field opposite the village of Pangboche. I got out and ran below the turning blades into the shelter of a stone wall to avoid the turbulence when he took off again. Seconds later he was a buzzing silver bee diminutive among the surrounding mountains and I was alone.

The sense of peace was uncanny. For weeks I had been among people who were never far off, often demanding, often giving of their warmth and friendship. Now I lay with my head resting on my rucksack, staring up at the blue sky where the midday cumulus was building up into a ruff round the base of Ama Dablam's needle peak that stood out pointing skywards. I was in a meadow a thousand feet (three hundred metres) above the valley, cut up by stone walls into a chessboard, and a few stone huts of the yakherds stood out like the chessmen. No sound disturbed the air. I was totally alone and but for the pain in my chest I would have been deeply content.

I suppose I passed a half-hour in dreaming about the big peaks around me, and I wondered what I was doing on a gigantic expedition such as this, despoiling the peace of the country like some devouring army.

My reveries were soon disturbed by the sound of the helicopter returning. It landed just long enough for me to dash under the revolving blades and climb in through a back door. I was hunched squatting on my rucksack in the luggage space with cold air vents playing on my back while the pilot and his doctor friend smoked Gauloises on either side of the Spaniard who was breathing oxygen. I pointed out the danger of explosion as tactfully as I could in sign language but this was met with a Gallic shrug of the shoulder.

I was past caring, my chest pain troubled me so. As we flew past Thyangboche the Spaniard had brightened up greatly and was panning the view with his ciné camera, proof of the immediate benefit of descending to lower altitude for a patient with acute mountain sickness.

By the time we reached Kathmandu the Spaniard had shed his oxygen mask and helmet and jumped out of the helicopter with a sprightly look on his bronzed face. He announced to the waiting press that it was all a fuss about nothing. Coming from a man who was only kept alive throughout the previous night by our oxygen, this was irony indeed. Furthermore, he later submitted a bill to the expedition for my share in the cost of the helicopter, oblivious of the fact that I had incurred the mischief in my chest working on his behalf.

At Shanta Bhawan Hospital I managed to sidestep the press, in whose minds some confusion existed as to who was the patient. I was taken aside by Dr. John Dickenson, who thoroughly examined me and took an x-ray. In his opinion the junction of the cartilage and bone of my eighth rib had separated and fractured under the stress of coughing and possibly a small spontaneous pneumothorax had developed that had been cured by blowing itself out with the descent to a lower altitude.

He put me to bed in a guest house in their garden and being inordinately weary I slept the clock round. During the next four days that I spent in Kathmandu the pain travelled along the course of my eighth rib to its junction with the spine where it settled, becoming daily less severe.

CHAPTER 7

My return to Kathmandu brought back memories of the year Sarah and I spent there in 1962 working in a missionary hospital. We were comfortably housed in an octagonal gambling den set in the imitation Japanese water garden of an old prince's palace, where we smuggled our beer in pillow cases and smoked in secret. Then the name Kathmandu evoked the most powerful sensations of adventure and oriental mystery. The temples, the bazaar, the colours, the smells were all new and every impression was vivid and exciting. The city has changed in the intervening years and now tourists throng the town, drugged hippies lounge glassy-eyed round the shrine of Swayambunath, taxis painted with yellow stripes like tigers whirl through the town slowed only by the new clockwork traffic lights and the cows that wander unmolested along the thoroughfares.

I recall vividly the excitement of my first view of the Himalayas, and am sad that never again can I revive the magical spontaneity with which I wrote about that experience soon after the monsoon clouds had lifted for the first time, revealing the snows:

I went for a stroll yesterday evening on the hill above the hospital. There is a large area of green meadow up there where the villagers go to graze their cattle, and plenty of trees. From the ridge you look down into big valley systems on both sides. To the south is Tansen, in a big basin of paddy fields ringed by hills and through a gap, stretching away into a haze, are the plains of the Ganges. Northwards are chain upon chain of foothills brilliantly clear, each ridge separated by deep rolling valleys, which makes a judgment of distance impossible. Wisps of cloud lay in some of the valleys, so distant hills were sitting on a shimmering mirage. The terraced rice fields, some full of water, some brilliant green with unplanted-out rice, run high up on the hillside where small groups of thatched sandy red brick houses are perched. Then beyond all this jungle wilderness a great wall of cloud, the monsoon that hangs over the Himalayas. But appearing like a fairy castle above the cloud a peak of Annapurna, majestic and shining white with the evening light full on it; I sat and watched as the cloud rolled away and showed the summit cone of Machapuchare, then Annapurna.

After four days' rest in Kathmandu I felt fit to return and was lucky to get a seat on a small Cessna plane flying in to Lukla. At the airport I met Boris Lissanevitch, the most fabled character in Kathmandu. Dressed in the open-necked holiday shirt that he always wears whether to entertain royalty or to hunt tigers, Boris beamed a friendly smile, "I will have fresh borscht and stroganoff dropped by parachute into the Western Cwm for your boys to climb on. That's what they need to be fit for Everest."

Previously patron of the Royal Hotel and more lately of the Yak and Yeti, Kathmandu's foremost eating-house, Boris Lissanevitch, through his spontaneous genius and unbridled generosity, has made and lost several fortunes and more than once landed himself in jail through unwittingly violating the law. But the renown of this former dancer in Diaghilev's Ballet Russe, champion game-hunter, art connoisseur, distiller and gourmet has spread across the world and he has become one of its most popular hosts.

His eyes twinkled and a mischievous grin spread across his face. "I'm off to Europe and my wife, Inger, is going to Khumbu to paint, so keep a look out for her," he said. "Your boys will get the borscht and stroganoff hot, we'll drop it in plastic containers, inside a water bag so it will bounce on the glacier and not burst. Then you will heat it and send it up the Face and that will get them to the top. A little vodka too may help on a cold night." Like many of his extravagant schemes this one, sadly, did not come off. Who can deny it might have been the crucial factor they were lacking that deprived the summit party of ultimate success?

The morning was perfectly clear and sitting beside the pilot of this light aircraft I was reminded of our air ambulance in Labrador, which was a Beaver, the toughest of all bush planes, equipped with floats in summer for landing on the many lakes or sea inlet harbours and with skis for the ice that gripped the coast and went deep into the interior for eight months of the winter. The engine noise was familiar, the checks, the dials, the movements of the controls. Small-airplane noises are frightening before one recognizes the meaning of each change of tone and realizes that the wings are not about to fall off.

From the cockpit window of the Cessna I could see a panorama across the entire length of the Himalayas, the greatest mountain barrier in the world. Peaks of immense size and beauty, beyond the experience and comprehension of many men less fortunate than I, rose serrated and fanged, sometimes carved in shapes of great delicacy, sometimes as crude, formless lumps of rock and ice. Flowing below us to the south the rivers cut deep ravines towards the distant plains and terraced fields climbed to the crests of the hillsides.

From the Beaver over Labrador the vistas were wide, wild and deserted and thereby more romantic; mile on mile of stunted pine forest was interspersed with a million lakes that cover more than two-thirds of the entire surface area of the region, much of which was frozen desert, the barren north, a land of intense desolation where universal whiteness was punctuated only by the tracks of deer, caribou, foxes and the many wild animals we would try to spot as we flew low over the trees and lakes.

Now we flew through a gap I recognized as a pass we had crossed a month before on the march-in. Straight ahead, Kanchenjunga rose above a line of cloud creeping up the valleys with advancing day. To our left the peaks of the Everest region were scattered at random and suddenly I saw Chomolungma (as Tibetans call Everest; to Nepalese it is Sagarmatha) itself, a gaunt triangular black face standing above its giant neighbours. It seemed hardly possible that our team would be struggling to reach the top of that peak during the next few weeks and I wondered about the fortunes, good and bad, that might befall us. What a strange thing to want to do, surrounded as we were by so much awesome beauty that commanded the eye just as much as that big peak of rock and ice where men had been before, where men had laboured fruitlessly and died for some uncertain end.

My philosophizing was brought to a sudden halt as I saw below us the landing strip of Lukla carved from a hillside on a shelf above the deep Dudh Kosi gorge. The pilot made a high circle, then he dropped down and flew level with the end of the runway, where he read the height of his altimeter for the approach; he made a shorter half-circle, keeping at exactly the same altitude, and then flew straight for the mountain side. The lip of the green strip of Lukla airfield appeared before us and we landed effortlessly and taxied up a steep ramp to where a Royal Nepal Army plane had lain for eighteen months like a crippled bird tilted on one side.

One policeman on permanent guard duty had moved with his family into the small house at the top end of the field and was now well and happily installed, his only work being to prevent inquisitive schoolchildren from using the plane as a climbing frame, grazing cows from scratching their backs on the underside of the wings and itinerant hippies from sleeping in it overnight. His uniform had not been pressed for many moons and in this sinecure, well away from watchful authority, he was truly content.

The Dudh Kosi valley had changed much in the month since we had passed by. Barrenness and austerity was replaced by greenery, flowers and warmth. Rhododendron trees had bloomed with rich scarlet flowers which gave a vivid colour to the valley; small purple primulae covered grassy banks on the sunward slopes; the tender green shoots of the willows and the pink cherry blossom told that spring had come.

I was alone, free and unencumbered, and so I sped on my way. Walking at speed on my own is one of the deepest joys I know; to carve a path through big country gives me a sense of achievement and pleasure. I was a little hampered by the pain in my chest that recurred if I breathed too deeply, but nevertheless I relished being by myself.

During the previous month I had enjoyed the novel experience of being a member of a team of remarkable people, but this was not my choice of living, not my style of travelling. I like to be in a small party, perhaps with a friend or two, even better with my family, roaming through mountains, living among the people so that one can truly get to know and understand them. We had been able to do this in Bhutan where the local people, who were even less used to Europeans than the Sherpas, accepted us as a travelling family, which was to them a natural phenomenon.

But in an expedition it is different. The sheer size of the party, the army of camp followers, makes it impracticable to stay in villagers' houses or travel incognito across the land.

The valley from Lukla to Namche makes one of the most beautiful Himalayan day's walking I know. At first the path stands high above the river, skirting creeks and bluffs and passing through small Sherpa villages whose stone-built houses have low-pitched, slatted pine roofs. Later on, river and track meet and run side by side up the length of a gorge whose walls climb precipitously, with trees growing from rocky ledges till the hilltops reach the sky; now and again a brief glance is caught of some snow-capped peak high above the valley.

I was wearing a pair of rubber-thonged sandals on my feet, something I had learnt from my wife, Sarah, who has always trekked in them, against the advice of well-wishing missionaries who insisted that a pair of sensible stout leather walking shoes would be more suitable. In fact I had sadly lost a most comfortable pair of suede boots that must have caught the fancy of a porter at one of our earlier camps.

My record with boots is a bad one. Two years previously I had left a new pair of climbing boots under the seat of a train taking me towards the mountains. Dorje, my Sherpa companion from Darjeeling, and I had dozed off to sleep in our carriage, having first removed our boots for comfort. At 3:30 a.m. we awoke with a start as the train was slowly drawing out of Samastapur Junction, where we had to change to a branch line for Jogbani on the Nepal border. We grabbed our rucksacks and dived out of the moving train as it was gathering speed from the station. I took a sad farewell of my boots from the platform where we stood, still half asleep. A helpful railwayman made urgent telephone calls down the line to the next station with a description of the pretty girl who shared the carriage (along with her parents) and who might have helped find the seat under which they lay. But I never recovered my boots. Some station coolie at Luknow was no doubt blessed with an oversize pair of new Vibrams with red laces — and who dares say that he doesn't deserve them more? Nevertheless I completed my journey in a pair of soft, comfortable desert boots and climbed two 19,000-foot (5,800-metre) peaks in them. So I had chosen to use the same footwear for the approach march this time and was well pleased until I lost them.

I stopped for a cup of tea in a dokan, a wayside house where travellers can refresh themselves with cups of sweet, stewed tea, occasionally get a meal of rice and chili-spiced potatoes and for little money hire a piece of floor space to sleep on. The road was busy as many hillmen from the south were returning home from Namche having sold their merchandise at the weekly market. With money in their pockets and chhang abundantly available at the dokans they were a merry bunch.

On the road I collected a young companion, Motilal by name, who asked if he might carry my camera. He pleaded he was an orphan, as do many children when tourists are about, and as he was going in the same direction to visit a relative farther up the valley I told him he could accompany me if he could keep up my pace. He was a ragged little ten-year-old from the neighbouring valley of Junbesi wearing a threadbare jacket, winkle-picker shoes with leather soles quite unsuited to mountain paths and a large black Nepali cap that rested on his ears. He stayed with me for a couple of hours and then left me to cross the river by a bridge, where I took a short rest in a meadow beside the river. The water bounded over rocks and into pools, taking breath before its next plunge into the sort of white foaming cataract that canoeists delight in. I had brought a medallion made from an old penny and inscribed "Bristol University Canoe Club," which I had promised to have placed as far up the mountain as possible. I have had many thrilling outings on the rivers of mid-Wales with the university boys and this river would have delighted them. As the path followed the valley upwards, the river, flowing in the opposite direction, gave a feeling of power and turbulence that one can only appreciate after experiencing the gripping excitement of trying to stay upright in rough water in a frail, unstable craft. Many times in weeks ahead I regretted that I had not stuck to canoeing with its wide margin of safety instead of endangering myself on such a crazy mountain as Everest.

Towards midday I reached the three bridges at the junction of the Bhote Kosi and the Dudh Kosi. From here the track takes to the cliff and climbs steeply through pine woods scented with juniper bushes and flowering shrubs towards Namche Bazaar.

I visited Ang Tsering's house, which stands beside the gompa over-looking the village. His family showed great pleasure that I had come and seated me beside the window on a low wooden bench covered with a brightly coloured Tibetan rug and plied me with cups of tea. In the far corner on the big family bed lay his mother, who suffers from tuberculo-sis of the spine and is almost bedridden.

"Welcome, Amji-La," she said, calling me by the Tibetan name for "doctor." "How is Ang Tsering?"

"Fine," I replied. "He's a good boy and he works well. He's learning a lot about medicine and is a big help."

"Please promise he won't climb the mountain, Amji-La, last year too many Sherpas were killed. We don't want it to happen again," the old lady said.

I had heard earlier that the Head Lama of Khumjung had prophesied that seventeen people would be killed on our expedition. Similar forecasts of his in the past have been uncannily accurate and this present prophecy did nothing to ease my own anxiety. Evidently the families of all the Sherpas, especially those of Namche from where the majority of last year's victims came, were acutely apprehensive about their menfolk.

Sherpas have become synonymous with high-altitude climbers, although the name is properly a racial subdivision of a people in Nepal similar to Bhotia, Tamang or Rai. Since the earliest days of Himalayan mountaineering Sherpas have proved themselves indispensable to any expedition. Surefooted on ice and snow, these truly natural mountaineers are acclimatized to live and work at altitude; strong as yaks and jovial as circus clowns, the praises of these little people of the high mountains have been sung by generations of climbers.

They live in a hard, unfruitful land where they scratch a living out of the poor soil, growing potatoes for their staple diet. They put their mountaineering talents to good use by hiring themselves as high-altitude porters. Not only can they carry heavy loads, more important in this form of climbing than alpine technique itself, but they are natural leaders and organizers. The British Army have never been able to use their services as mercenary soldiers in the Gurkha regiments because the Sherpas, being Buddhists, are forbidden by their faith to kill living creatures; thereby the army has been denied a race of first-class non-commissioned officers.

Now the Sherpas are in good business. The number of expeditions has increased, many more people are trekking in the mountains of Nepal and the Sherpas' qualities fit them well for this kind of work. Yet they still have to hire themselves out at less than a pound a day to perform heavy, tedious and often dangerous work on the mountains in order to put their hirer in a position to climb some summit in which they themselves have no particular interest. It must be very mystifying for them to see others with apparently unlimited money, supplies and equipment coming in large parties to scale their mountains — and to what end? Frequently there is loss of life — more often among the Sherpas than their employers. On Everest alone more than twenty Sherpas have died. The surprising fact is that they perform their duties with such good grace and humour.

During recent years prospects for the Sherpas have improved and no one has more thanks due to him than Sir Edmund Hillary, whose fame was made possible by their help, which he has amply repaid. At the time Everest was climbed for the first time in 1953 by the British team, it was sad but inevitable, with modern publicity, that individuals had to be picked out for glory. The achievement was the climax of a team effort whereby any one of Evans, Bourdillon, Noyce, Lowe, Hunt — all brilliant climbers — was equally qualified to be the man for the summit. The chance fell to Edmund Hillary and he seized it with both hands and brought off success. Fame followed and his name and Sherpa Tenzing Norgay's became known by millions of schoolchildren across the world.

Hillary has ploughed his assets back into the land of the Sherpas, where he is now held with a reverence equal to that of the high lamas. Under his aegis, expeditions of his fellow New Zealanders have built bridges, three at the junction of the two rivers below Namche; they have laid pipes to lead water from springs outside Khumjung and Phortse to the centre of the village; at Kunde they have built a hospital that is staffed by a New Zealand doctor under their overseas volunteer program; and schools have been built at Khumjung, Thami, Thyangboche, Pangboche, Phortse, and others are in preparation at Junbesi and Beding in the Rolwaling Valley beyond the Tesi Lapcha pass. Much of Hillary's time is spent travelling to collect money for his enterprises and his forthright approach at luncheons of American businessmen has rarely failed to produce the cash.

Any sneaking doubts I may have entertained about individual members of that 1953 team being singled out for knighthoods disappeared after seeing these results, which could never have been financed without the renown that Edmund Hillary gained from climbing Everest on that historic May 29. As a schoolboy I stood guard on the Victoria Memorial outside Buckingham Palace on Coronation morning and I well remember seeing the newspaper headlines — "All this and Everest too" — and the burning pride that I felt then.

With these thoughts wandering through my mind I gazed out of the window of Ang Tsering's house while his wife made tea. I could see some women tilling the terraced fields in the centre of the village, through which a good-sized stream flows. The only men to be seen were the old ones who were past expedition work.

Inside the house people were gathering to see the new arrival. An old blind grandmother was led up the dark staircase into the large upper room where we sat. She had dense cataracts in both eyes and I volunteered to operate on her after the expedition was over, a suggestion the old lady accepted with surprising alacrity and gratitude. I did the operation on my way out and she now has good sight with her new spectacles.

All Sherpa houses are built in a similar style, which is helpful for finding one's way around in the darkness. The walls are built with well-dressed dry stone. Down the valley in the hill country of the Rais and Limbus the houses are quite different in character, having mud-plastered walls, red below the first floor and limewashed white above, and the roofs are thatched with grass. In Sherpa houses a wooden staircase leads from the ground floor cattle bower to the first floor and in one corner at the top of the stairs, or in a small adjoining room, a hole is made in the floor for use as a latrine. A supply of pine needles and dried leaves is kept in a basket beside the hole and these are thrown over the excrement, abolishing all smell and at the same time producing a very useful supply of compost.

The large single upstairs room has a baked earth fireplace with two or three openings for pots, or alternatively there may be an open iron basket grate. Along the walls wooden benches are set with low tables in front of them and in a far corner large wooden chests hold the bedding. On the opposite wall are strong shelves on which large copper pots for keeping water and chhang are placed. Their number, size and ornamentation are a mark of affluence among Sherpa housewives. The windows are small and have sliding shutters which admit only a little light. The darkness of the room is accentuated by the walls and ceiling being blackened by tar from the woodsmoke which continually hangs in the room despite the open chimney above the fire. Commonly the swastika motif is seen painted in white lime patterns on the dark beams. In the recess for the family bed are shelves for the family treasures, cooking utensils and a gallery of photographs of their men taken on expeditions over the years.

I enjoyed the conviviality in Ang Tsering's home and as more relatives came in the arak began to flow freely and the party became more and more rowdy. I was glad when rice and curried yak meat arrived as my head was reeling with so much alcohol drunk on an empty stomach. After eating well I drank several cups of Tibetan tea made by brewing bricks of leaves and then churning it up with butter and salt using a plunger in a long wooden cylinder. Tea was served in a walnut wood cup lined with silver, standing on a small silver pedestal and with an embossed silver lid.

As a result of the elaborate hospitality I staggered slowly up the hill from the village towards Kunde, where I planned to stay the night. Selwyn Lang and his wife Ann, both of them doctors, had been running the small hospital at Kunde for more than a year. They had become well established and had gained a favourable reputation among the Sherpas. We talked till late that night.

"If you ever need an extra pair of hands in an emergency I'd be pleased to help," said Selwyn and I was glad to have this reassurance. Although not claiming to be a mountaineer he had proved himself a powerful walker, marching from Kathmandu to Namche in five and a half days, a journey that normally takes eleven.

Next morning I left early as I wanted to reach Base Camp the same day. I sped through the winding paths of Kunde village, down past the potato fields of Khumjung and the chorten that guards the entrance to the valley, and plunged into the woods which fall steeply towards the Dudh Kosi. The sun was warm and a delicious smell came from the pine trees, where resin was oozing from the bark and fir cones and pine needles lay on the ground. Bushes in the undergrowth contrasted in colour, and small primulae with many-headed flowers on long stalks grew in damp hollows.

After crossing the bridge I stopped for a cup of tea at a dokan beside some little temples built astride a stream that powered the prayer wheels housed inside them. Prayers are written on thousands of pieces of paper and put inside big drums which are colourfully painted with the sacred words *Om mane padme hum* picked out in gold. From the base of the upright cylinder a rod projects vertically downwards with four paddles attached to it. As water flows onto the paddles it turns them and the big drum revolves, striking a bell with each revolution; thus prayers are cast off into the ether perpetually. Similarly, faithful Buddhists hold small prayer wheels in the hand and spin them with a rhythmical swing of the wrist, assisted by a ball weight on a chain, as they recite their sacred texts. Prayers are also printed by means of wooden block dies on long flags which are then attached to high poles. As they flutter in the wind, prayers are sped away across the distant mountains that are the embodiment of the power of the deity the Sherpas and Tibetans worship, and a spiritual force in their lives.

As I began the long climb towards Thyangboche I joined company with a Sherpa who was walking from Namche to attend his yaks grazing at Pangboche. He plied me with rakshi but I did not like the fellow at all as he was drunk and abusive. Namche people have a reputation in the Khumbu for roughness of tongue and behaviour (though our expedition Sherpas from there were far from typical in this respect). Namche has always been a trading post and perhaps the atmosphere of tough bargaining has made them as unpopular as they are successful in business. The Tibetans who settle there are of a rugged breed; apparently when the Sherpas used to cross the Nangpa La north to trade in Tibet they travelled with their knives in their hands in constant fear of brigands who hailed rocks down on them from the mountains above the road.

I quickly strode ahead of my lurching acquaintance and an hour later passed through a gatehouse built across the path, ornately decorated inside with paintings of the life and teaching of Lord Buddha. I came out onto an open sward of meadow in front of Thyangboche Monastery, perhaps the most beautifully situated group of buildings in the world. The burnt-ochre and dun-red walls of the gompa are surmounted by a wide-eaved, pagoda-shaped roof with a central golden lantern. Smaller whitewashed buildings spread out to form the base of a pyramid in the foreground.

Beyond, the valley rises past Pangboche towards the 6000-foot (1,800-metre) wall of Nuptse, serrated with ice gullies which cut diagonally

South-West face of Everest

Himalayan peak

Wayside dokan or teahouse

Yaks below Pumori

Resting beside a chorten

Chorten and prayer flags

Clinic for porters

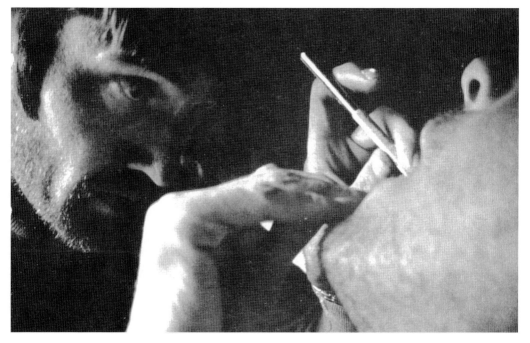

Mobile dentistry (JOHN CLEARE)

Tibetan porter

Sherpani porter

Sherpa grandmother

Namche schoolgirl

Sherpanis on bridge

Porter crossing bridge

Yaks at Thyangboche

Tibetan yak driver

Pheriche village

Base Camp

Sherpa sirdar Pembatharkay

Base Camp hospital (JOHN CLEARE)

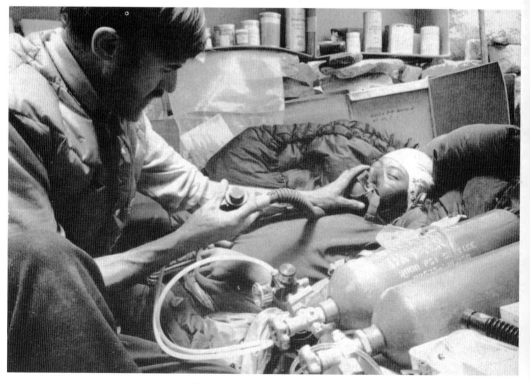

Giving oxygen to a sick Spaniard

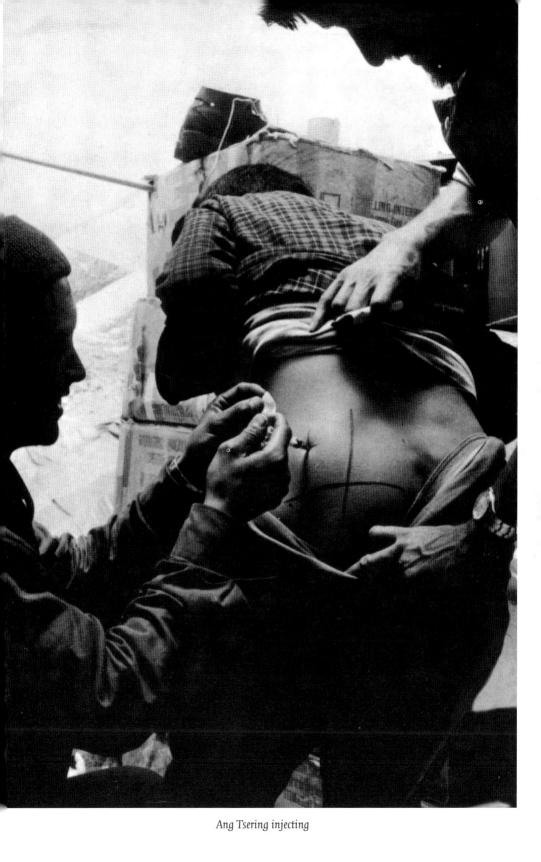

Ang Tsering injecting

International flags over Base Camp

Carlo Mauri

Don Whillans

across the face in many directions yet leave it blank, featureless and ugly. The summit of Everest peeps over the middle of the wall, its true size masked as one sees only the final two thousand feet (six hundred metres) of the Southwest Face. "Strange to think that Don and Dougal could be up there in a month," I wrote in my diary.

In the chhang house where I stopped for a brief rest I met Sonam (Sen) Tenzing, Eric Shipton's old Sherpa, in whose house I had stayed two years before when I was exploring a valley on the way towards Cho Oyu. He greeted me warmly and we exchanged news of mutual friends. Eric Shipton called him "the Foreign Sportsman" as he used to stride around Darjeeling with the swagger of a modern alpine guide, fully kitted out in his new boots and climbing clothes before setting off on an expedition. He had been with Shipton and Tilman the first time the Nanda Devi Sanctuary was entered in 1935.

Sonam, who has strong religious convictions, was at Thyangboche to bring an offering to the Head Lama of the monastery. On our way through the expedition had been given an audience by this holy man. Norman Dyhrenfurth had announced, "At 2 p.m. tomorrow we are meeting the high lama of Thyangboche."

"T'd be a lot easier t'bring 'im down 'ere," grumbled Don Whillans.

We did, however, go and we presented him with donations of money for the monastery building and he blessed the expedition in the same way as his counterpart across the mountain range at Rongbuk Monastery used to bless the pre-war expeditions approaching Mount Everest through Tibet. Dave Peterson and I gave him a selection of flower and vegetable seeds from America, which gave him great pleasure and should grow well at these altitudes if the strains are carefully selected. When travelling light on previous journeys I had found difficulty in knowing what to give as presents in return for hospitality; this is an established custom in the Buddhist world. Colourful calendars of Britain were heavy but popular and provided a good talking point. I finally decided the best presents were coloured ballpoint pens, packets of heavy gauge surgical needles, sets of poker dice and a variety of packets of seeds.

I deeply admire Buddhism as a practical faith; many of its precepts and practices are noticeably similar to Catholicism. But the lamaist system is liable to the same abuses of power as are evident in the Church in Latin America. Bhutan is an exclusively lamaistic country and we formed the impression that religion was promoted for the benefit of the priesthood rather than the laity. But if those who administer the faith are at fault, the faith itself is not invalidated. Tibetan Buddhists are extraordinarily tolerant, a quality rarely found in ardent Christians, and this tolerance adds to their strength.

From the monastery above I heard the faithful being summoned by a gong, which was an empty oxygen bottle from a former expedition hanging by a string from the balcony.

I walked through the beech woods below Thyangboche on my way up the valley and passed through the village of Dawa Tensing, an old Everest "Tiger" and Charles Evans' sirdar on many Himalayan journeys. I had not intended to stop but merely to pay my respects in passing. However, he insisted I went upstairs for some refreshment despite my assurances that I was not in need of it. Dawa produced his Himalayan Society book with commendations in the handwriting of Rutledge, Finch, Tilman, Shipton, Houston, Hunt, Evans and Hillary, a precious and unique document of mountaineering history of which he was immensely and rightfully proud.

I was overloaded with fluid on leaving his house and set off at a fast walk up the Imja Khola to make up the time I had lost on these pleasant digressions. Not long after I met the drunken Sherpa of my earlier acquaintance lying on his back with one arm across his face and an empty rakshi bottle beside him. I thought I had better wake him as he might make things rough for me later if I passed him by, as I was at first keen to do. He awoke and lurched along the path with an idiotic drunken grin and unsteady gait. As we were in a narrow place where the river dashed into a gorge and was crossed by a small bridge, I thought I ought to escort him for a while to see he did not fall from the bridge or take a step off the steep mountain path that levelled as we approached

Pangboche. I got rid of him by persuading him to rest by a chorten and say his prayers.

Beyond Pangboche I rose above the tree line and enjoyed the open moorland country before the path cut into the steep cliffside on the left bank of the river, which raced southwards a thousand feet below. At midday I reached a bridge at the junction of two valleys, that to the right goes up the Imja glacier towards Makalu and Baruntse while the left one, after several devious turns, leads to Everest.

I arrived at Pheriche, where we had pitched our acclimatization camp some weeks before, and entered the first house in the village, which was an excellent dokan where we had spent a pleasant evening drinking chhang. The very handsome Sherpani proprietor, whose husband Mingmo I knew from my previous visit, prepared some food for me to eat; I lay down in my sleeping bag and was dead to the world for the ensuing hour. I am fortunate in my ability to benefit from cat naps. Ordinarily I wake in the middle of the night when something is on my mind and have difficulty in going to sleep again, but I can sit in a chair after a meal, become deeply unconscious for a few minutes and awake refreshed and alert after my brief excursion into that delicious land of dreams.

The dokan had one single room with a barn attached and a roof of turf sods. An open fireplace stood at one end, partitioned off for the family by a flimsy board papered with pages of an old Life magazine. Low scrub bushes that grow on the valley floor are burned instead of firewood, and produce a dense pall of acrid smoke that hangs under the ceiling of the house. The only way to avoid inhaling the smoke that provoked an irritating cough and made tears flow from the eyes was to lie on the floor. Soot stuck to the roof timbers and clung to the cobwebs like black stalactites.

My hostess squatted beside the fire preparing rice in a dekchi, an aluminium cooking pot, and frying potatoes with chopped chives in an iron pan. She cut some yak meat from a dried quarter that was hanging in one corner and fried it with chili sauce. She managed these complicated cooking manoeuvres at the same time as she breast-fed her chubby year-old baby.

Opposite the village of Pheriche is Taweche, a small but handsome peak of 22,000 feet (6,700 metres). From the valley floor a long ice gully rises up 2,000 feet (600 metres) of its lower slopes towards a shoulder before the final steep ramp that cuts across the face of the mountain. I had a good view of the whole gully and thought back to the day I had climbed it with Dougal Haston a month before.

I marched up the valley, still rejoicing in being alone, and big snowflakes fell from the darkening sky as I started the long climb towards Lobuje. Still I was going strongly and had almost forgotten the pain in my chest.

I reached Lobuje at three o'clock in the afternoon and snow was falling thickly; the clouds had come right down to the valley and dirty weather had set in. I thought it would be unwise to push on and try to reach Base Camp that night so I entered a stone hut that passes for a hotel and drank tea, ate some rice and settled down on the floor for the night.

Next morning was clear as I set off along the path that clings to the left-hand side of the Khumbu moraine. The storm of the previous night had left a thin covering of snow on the ground, making the path difficult to follow. After an hour I met Khunjo Chumbi, the village headman. He wore dark sunglasses under a broad-brimmed trilby hat and a long, belted, sheepskin-lined overcoat which almost reached to the ground, just showing his white gym shoes. He smiled broadly and his little drooping moustache, worn after the fashion of the Chinese mandarins, gave him the look of the oriental potentate that in a small way he is.

He has danced in Paris night clubs, stood at the top of the Empire State Building, been photographed with Beefeaters at the Tower of London and dined with geisha girls in Tokyo. All this and more happened on his world tour with the alleged scalp of the Yeti (afterwards thought to be a bit of old goat hide) that is kept in the gompa at Khumjung. He was accompanied by Sir Edmund Hillary on this tour, which was arranged at the end of the 1961 Yeti-hunting expedition.

The Yeti and the Loch Ness Monster have certain features in common. As a tourist attraction they are too important for the myths ever to be allowed to die. I like to believe in the Yeti in the same way as I do in the Monster; in this age when everything has a scientific explanation I enjoy a phenomenon that is inexplicable and charged with mystery.

In 1962 I had crossed a pass about 16,000 feet (4,900 metres) high while exploring Hiunchuli Patan and in the snow I found a line of regularly spaced twelve-inch-long (30-centimetre) footprints which went for about forty yards and then disappeared onto rock. My Sherpas told me they belonged to the Yeti and they became quite scared. They assured me in all seriousness that if we met the Yeti we must throw lighted matches in his face and this would frighten him away. I am quite prepared to believe that the prints belonged to the Abominable Snowman; they looked remarkably similar to those photographed by Eric Shipton on the 1951 Everest reconnaissance expedition. People have frequently reported seeing the Yeti since. Don Whillans speaks with the utmost seriousness of seeing it on Annapurna last year, but I am assured by reliable witnesses that he had consumed several "jars" that night. For people running short of excuses to visit the Himalayas, when trumped-up scientific programs no longer impress the bodies that hold the purse strings the Yeti will always be there — and I hope they never catch him.

I delivered to Khunjo Chumbi some stomach pills that Dr. Selwyn Lang had entrusted to me, and after an affable conversation with the rascally-looking old man I walked on, glad of his footprints in the snow to guide me on the right path.

After an hour I reached Gorak Shep and tried to get some tea from some coolies who were sleeping in a small stone hut. They were all lying side by side under some yak-hair blankets and my presence caused much confusion among the women in their party as Sherpas sleep naked and no one dared move to prepare the fire for tea. I left, allowing them to retain their modesty, as I knew it would be a long time before the tea would be ready.

Some yak drivers had slept the night at Gorak Shep and had departed a little while before me on their way to Base Camp, carrying stores and firewood. Following the yaks' tracks I caught up with them at the beginning of Phantom Alley, where the path leaves the moraine and winds its way up the Khumbu glacier through the contorted maze of ice pinnacles.

The caravan of yaks ahead of me made a most picturesque sight. The bells around their necks, tied on with wide webbing straps and scarlet bobbles, rang out, breaking the still quiet of the valley. To spur them across difficult sections of path the drivers throw stones, which bounce innocuously off their heavy coats, and shout "encouraging words" as Bailey naïvely said, writing about his early travels in Bhutan and Sikkim; in fact, the meaning would offend the ears of any well-brought-up yak.

The yak is a magnificent beast; beautiful as Highland cattle, with sensuously curved horns, long, shaggy hair that hangs almost to the ground like an outsize coat and is especially thick on the rump and tail, and feet as sure on steep rocky ground as the chamois'. He is also the universal provider on the uplands of Tibet, his native home. Yak's hair is woven to make cloth; meat and milk provide food; dung is dried in cakes and used for fuel; and he carries loads over the rough high passes in weather conditions that no other beast could tolerate. It is a delight to see yaks standing in the moonlight with the temperature well below zero, their breath freezing on their hairy mouths, awaiting the warmth of the rising sun.

Before nine o'clock I saw the orange tents of Base Camp standing out clearly against the surrounding grey, white and black, and was back with the expedition again after my pleasant digression.

CHAPTER 8

W ork was moving ahead steadily and pairs of climbers were going up daily, making the route safer by changing its course to avoid dangerous seracs, strengthening crevasse bridges and adding sections of fixed rope so that it would be safe for the big lift of men and supplies into the Western Cwm that was about to begin.

The condition of the Icefall this year was the worst in anyone's memory. I think many of the party were apprehensive about it, though few voiced their opinion in public. But their fears came through in the interviews that Antony Thomas, the producer of the BBC film unit, had with each member early on in the expedition:

> "The real danger, which is completely out of our hands, is that we may have established a safe route through the Icefall, but as the season goes on and the weeks go by the glacier alters. This may become dangerous from an Icefall collapse, and there's nothing you can do if you're on the spot at the time."

"The main danger is the Khumbu Icefall where towers can turn over and walls can fall down on you, and perhaps also the wind on the West Ridge, but I don't think that will be such a problem as the Icefall."

"The objective danger is the Icefall itself over which we have no control except to plan our route as safely as we possibly can. There certainly is a possibility that I can get killed in the next two months and I am sure everyone on the team realizes the same fact, but I don't feel particularly apprehensive."

"I fear the height, the lack of oxygen and the cold; the worst I think happens when I freeze my fingers or my toes."

"To a slight degree the Icefall worries me but I don't think this is too bad."

"I guess my greatest fear right now is the Icefall, which has played something of a role in my mind."

"I don't think there is any place for fear on a mountain like this. There is rockfall, avalanche, wind and cold, everything that could make you scared, but I guess the ultimate fear — the fear of death — is something that I've made peace with."

The first men to go into the Icefall on March 24 were Naomi Uemura of Japan and Carlo Mauri of Italy along with the British pair Don Whillans and Dougal Haston. Don found he was still troubled with dizziness and vertigo that had started at Pheriche and he came down to rest; his place was taken by Leo Schlömmer.

During the next days the Austrian Wolfgang Axt and Harsh Bahuguna from India took a party of Sherpas up into the Icefall carrying long logs to reinforce the bridges and so make crossing the crevasses safer. Odd Eliassen and his Norwegian compatriot Jon Teigland pushed on beyond

Dump Camp, where Michel Vaucher from Switzerland had camped the previous night with some Sherpas, and they discovered a huge crevasse at the top of the fall where ice begins to spill over a sill and pour down off the mountain, breaking up on its way.

David Peterson and Reizo Ito of Japan were strengthening the crevasse bridges and wire ladders in the middle section.

"Man, it's just beautiful," said Dave. "You've never seen anything so dangerous. It's just as if an atomic bomb has exploded up there."

The dangers of the Icefall were becoming increasingly apparent and early exuberant accounts of its beauty were giving way to a more sober realization of the ever-present perils, which were especially marked in the upper section. David Isles (U.S.A.) was leading a rope of six Sherpas when part of an ice wall above their path collapsed a few seconds after they had gone by, pitching one ladder into a crevasse and dislodging three others.

"This sort of incident tends to make you thoughtful," remarked David with characteristic understatement not typical of his nation. Most concern was caused by a wall that leant over several degrees above the path for a space of a hundred yards and could not be avoided. The Sherpas were so frightened of the place they scattered votive offerings of rice on the ground to propitiate the gods for the safety of their passage and hurried up through the ominous shadow the wall cast across their path murmuring their prayers, "Om mane padme hum." It became known as the "mane wall" thereafter and mention of it never ceased to elicit a shudder of fear.

The pairing in the Icefall sorties was quite haphazard and the international spirit was exemplary. It would be difficult to imagine any mountaineering party having a more happy and friendly start. None of the undercurrents that one hears of in the unpublished accounts of so many expeditions had been manifest, though so far nothing very challenging had taxed the goodwill of members of the party.

On March 31, Harsh Bahuguna and Reizo Ito pushed over the top of the Icefall and found the site for Camp I. On April 3, Camp I was pitched on a huge wall of ice that stood free from the main glacier. It measured a mere thirty feet (nine metres) wide and a crevasse a hundred feet (thirty metres) deep lay on its upper side; the ground below sloped into another crevasse that was so profound one could only peer into its dark recesses, unable to see the bottom. Nearby at the entrance to the Cwm a narrow snow bridge lay diagonally across the wide crevasse that had blocked the advance of Eric Shipton's reconnaissance party in 1951 and was crossed with much difficulty by a rope bridge in the 1952 Swiss expedition.

A party consisting of Reizo Ito, Harsh Bahuguna, Carlo Mauri, Dougal Haston and Don Whillans, with five Sherpas, entered the Western Cwm on April 5. Don, looking like Father Christmas going off to deliver his gifts, was loaded up with bamboo marker flags. They pushed right on to the head and on April 6 found a site for Camp II, the Advance Base Camp, at the very far end close to the foot of the Southwest Face of the mountain. The following day Dougal Haston and Don Whillans began looking for a way up the lower part of the Face.

Meanwhile I sat at Base Camp following the progress of the advance towards the mountain over the radio. Lil Bahadur, the operator, had a tent of his own and at the time of a scheduled contact many people would crowd into it and sit on boxes or rolls of bedding to hear the latest news of progress.

I was very busy at this time. Many of the Sherpas were suffering from bronchitis and broncho-pneumonia and my evening clinic was full of coughing, hawking men, many of whom were genuinely ill; others thought it would be good to have a few days' rest from the arduous, boring and dangerous business of humping heavy loads up through the Icefall. Ang Tsering was now skilled at giving injections and we used intramuscular penicillin for treating the Sherpas, as one could never be sure that tablets prescribed were not swapped or sold to their fellows. Clinics were jovial times when much banter and joking went on and I enjoyed them.

As Sherpas were soon going to start carrying loads up through the Icefall, some instruction in the basic techniques of ice climbing was held on the glacier a few minutes from camp, where some steep little ice slopes made a suitable spot to practise walking on crampons and getting used to the feel of being roped.

Dougal Haston took charge of this instruction and Harsh Bahuguna and I went to help interpret for those who could not understand English. Harsh had a particular sympathy for the Sherpas who in their turn liked and respected him; they were hillmen similar to those soldiers he had commanded as a major in the Indian Army. He climbed much in Garwhal, the Himalayan territory of India which lies on Nepal's western border. He was a thorough soldier, from his clean-cut handsome looks to his firm disciplinarian approach to his subordinates.

Harsh worked very hard in the early stages of the expedition, easing our thirty tons of equipment through the Indian Customs at Bombay with the help of John Evans and Duane Blume, who had accompanied one part by sea from America, the other part having arrived on an Italian boat from Europe. This job required tact and authority such as Harsh was able to bring, and he also needed to ensure that no one tried to be awkward and hold up the clearance, as had happened to so many previous expeditions.

Harsh had climbed exclusively in the Himalayas and in 1965, with the successful Indian expedition to Mount Everest, had reached more than 28,000 feet (8,500 metres) before he had been forced to turn back. I confess I found difficulty in understanding why he should wish to return to the mountain having been through it all once before. But he threw himself into the expedition with the keenness of a first-timer and was recognized as a tireless worker and a completely unselfish man. He became close friends with John Evans on the march-in and they were an example to any of us who felt like soft-pedalling.

Harsh Bahuguna could also be tough, and one night when two French hippies pitched their tent in the middle of Base Camp he told them in terms that left no doubt as to his meaning what they should do with their tent and instructed the Sherpas, with a vehemence that took many people by surprise, to see them off down the valley.

I have met quite a number of Indian soldiers and find them smart, professional and highly disciplined. Harsh possessed all these qualities and with his politeness and friendliness he became a universally liked member of the expedition from the very beginning. I came to know him

during the walk-in because he was very anxious about his health; he had
suffered from cracked lips before on Everest and did not want such a constant source of discomfort to happen again. He strained his knee and was
worried lest it should weaken on the mountain and he could not get rid
of an irritating sore throat. This was the sign not of mere hypochondria,
but of a sincere concern that he should be in top trim on the mountain.

I think Harsh recognized his own inexperience in advanced alpine
climbing techniques compared with many of the professionals in the
expedition, but his knowledge of the Himalayas singled him out to be sent
ahead to choose the site for Base Camp along with Naomi Uemura, who
had also been there before. He was one of the first men into the Icefall,
where he paired up and developed a close friendship with Wolfgang Axt.

Harsh's two daughters were the same age as my own older children
and we had some long talks about our family life — something that meant
a great deal to us both. We composed birthday telegrams for our children
and Lance-Corporal Lil Bahadur Gurung, the radio operator seconded to
the expedition from the 17th Gurkha Signals, transmitted them on his set
direct to Kathmandu.

Harsh was deeply religious and always carried on him a small statue
of Ganapati, the Hindu god of good fortune. He lost this early on in the
expedition and this worried him a lot. He wrote in his diary, "I searched all
over but could not find it. My morale went terribly low."

The ice-work practice went ahead with Dougal Haston leading a line
of Sherpas across a steep slope with deceptive ease and gracefulness
more reminiscent of a dancer than of a mountaineer. I followed up in the
rear and Harsh Bahuguna stood below, shouting orders to them: "Keep
all the points of your crampons on the ice. Stand straight up, don't lean
in towards the slope. Mind the coils of your rope."

In characteristic Sherpa fashion they found great amusement in the
exercise, especially when one of them slipped and slithered twenty feet
(six metres) down the slope, landing in an ungainly heap at the bottom.
Many were novices, others were old hands at the game. Pembatharkay,
who had been on Annapurna and was devoted to both Dougal Haston

and Don Whillans, assumed the position of instructor. He was a very strong man with a firm, square jaw pointing forward, who had aspirations of going high on the Face.

All the Sherpas had new equipment and looked smart in their blue pullovers with red and white bands on each arm. Some were destined to become high-altitude Sherpas, the cream of the team; those still doing their apprenticeship would serve in the Icefall as porters, a job as tedious as it was dangerous. But even after only one afternoon's instruction they rapidly got the feeling for the technique and were itching to get onto the mountain.

Despite my enjoyment of solitude during my walk up the valley in the preceding days I was pleased to be back among my friends at Base Camp. The Icefall route had just been completed and Michel Vaucher and Naomi Uemura had occupied Camp I the night before I arrived and were moving on into the Western Cwm. The activity and excitement around Base Camp was intense and everyone was preparing to move up and begin the big lift of supplies towards the mountain.

With the way through the Icefall open, the Face team and the West Ridge team began to take on separate identities in a way that had not been necessary before. In effect the leaders were attempting to mount two quite separate expeditions on the mountain, and this accounted for the large number of men and materials involved and the need for each to be a self-contained entity.

Because so many potential leaders were present among the two groups the term "climbing leader" was dropped and each team had a "coordinator," John Evans for the Face and Wolfgang Axt for the West Ridge. The final composition of the teams is as shown at the top of the next page.

Some changes had taken place since people had been asked, in a letter from Norman Dyhrenfurth some time before leaving Europe, to state their preference for the routes. Both Carlo Mauri and Pierre Mazeaud had originally been chosen for the Face but now asked to join the Ridge team.

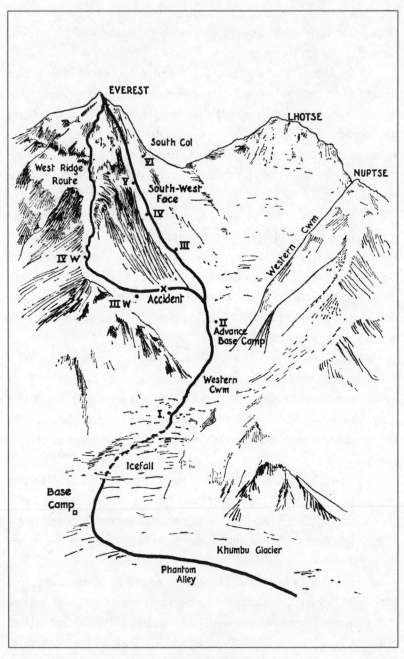

Mount Everest from the south

Face	*West Ridge*
John Evans (U.S.A.)	Wolfgang Axt (Austria)
Gary Colliver (U.S.A.)	Harsh Bahuguna (India)
Dougal Haston (U.K.)	Odd Eliassen (Norway)
Toni Hiebeler (W. Germany)	David Isles (U.S.A.)
Reizo Ito (Japan)	Carlo Mauri (Italy)
David Peterson (U.S.A.)	Pierre Mazeaud (France)
Leo Schlömmer (Austria)	Jon Teigland (Norway)
Naomi Uemura (Japan)	Michel Vaucher (Switzerland)
Don Whillans (U.K.)	Yvette Vaucher (Switzerland)
	Peter Steele (U.K.)

I found myself included as a member of the West Ridge team with some surprise and delight. I had originally accepted the invitation from Norman on the understanding that I was not expected to go high on the mountain. The doctor on the Face was to be David Peterson, who could go up in case of emergency; I would remain at Advance Base Camp.

I think my inclusion in the climbing team came about like this: I was going very strongly on the march-in and had become friendly with the predominantly French-speaking continental group who mainly composed the Ridge team. As I speak tolerable French I was adopted as their interpreter.

After my gully climb at Pheriche with Dougal Haston people suddenly realized I could climb a little, although I would not pretend that I had ever, even in my best climbing days some years back, approached anywhere near their standard. But the Ridge team made it quite clear I was one of their number and that they intended to take me as high as possible. As both they and Norman Dyhrenfurth expressed the hope that, given good conditions and reasonable luck, the whole Ridge team might reach the top, I became excited at the sudden realization I had never previously entertained, that I might be given a chance to climb high on the mountain. I never wrote of this to Sarah for fear of worrying her, but at that time when I was feeling strong and going like a steam train I felt exceedingly pleased and proud.

My sudden chest trouble had worried me greatly as I was afraid that it might prevent my going high, so I was pleased to have had such a thorough check in Kathmandu and to find that nothing serious was wrong.

THE TWO TEAM coordinators were different in every way: background, temperament and experience.

John Evans had the most powerful physique of any man on the expedition; with his huge barrel-chest and bulging muscles, crew-cut hair, freckled face, clicking speech when pronouncing the letter "S" and his ready smile he was the prototype all-American college boy. He had recently been working as an electronics engineer on the American space program.

John's expedition record is impressive; two visits to Antarctica, climbs in New Zealand and many very hard routes in America and Alaska. He was described to Norman Dyhrenfurth by one of the most distinguished modern American climbers as "the very best type of expedition guy." If any dirty work had to be done John was in the thick of it and he was always the last to leave a camp site, having scoured it for rubbish and litter. Although by no means the best or most experienced climber, it was no chance choice that he was coordinator of the Face team.

His enthusiasm for all the newness and beauty we encountered was infectious. One memorable evening in Kathmandu we cycled out to the house of a Tibetan friend of mine, Lobsang Tinling, to celebrate Tashi Delek, the Tibetan Lhosar festival. We ate momo and drank arak through bamboo pipes, seated on ornate and colourful carpets. With the strong drink John became increasingly loquacious about these strange and exciting surroundings. Late at night we mounted our bicycles and made an erratic and perilous descent without lights in total darkness, from Tinling's house, laughing inanely as we crashed through potholes and narrowly missing riding into sacred cows asleep in the middle of the road.

Wolfgang Axt, an Austrian mathematics schoolteacher from the village of St. Johann, Pongau, is an alpinist of wide experience and horizon. His expeditions have taken him far afield to the Karakoram Himalayas, to the top of Mount Elbruz in the Caucasus range, to explore in Arctic Spitzbergen, to Mount Ararat in Turkey, to Peru, where he climbed thirty peaks of more than 16,000 feet (5,000 metres) in one season, and recently to the Hindu Kush, where he led an Austrian party.

Wolfgang had a reputation as a health enthusiast — an aspect of him I encountered early on. We shared a room together for one night in Calcutta. Having slept little during the previous night on the plane, I lay down to rest in a room with the curtains drawn and the fan blowing sensuous cooling air over my naked body. I opened an eye and, through a vague fog of half awakening, I saw in the air a pair of feet moving around the room, making me wonder if the world had turned upside down. However, looking more closely I realized that Wolfgang was walking on his hands as part of his daily exercises. After thirty knee bends balancing on one foot and a similar number of press ups (changing to one hand after ten) he sat on the edge of the bed, small beads of sweat gleaming on his bronzed, brawny torso on which the veins stood out from the muscle contours like an anatomical sketch by Leonardo da Vinci.

Wolfgang offered me a bottle, "Rub on the chest, it is good for the lungs you know — to keep out the cold."

I looked at my pallid form and accepted the herbal unction. "Thanks, Wolfgang."

"Now this one for the feet to make them strong," he said, delving into his wash bag, which was like a physician's pharmacopoeia. "Did you bring any acclimatization medicine?"

"No, it's a load of old rubbish. Just a lot of vitamins put together under a fancy trade name," I said. Wolfgang was appalled, and I realized my casualness was not appreciated. This was to blow back on me a couple of weeks later on the march-in, when one evening the iron (termed "I–ron") tablets that were put out at meal times for each person to take were thrown away by an overzealous kitchen worker making a clean sweep of the table.

"The iron tablets are lost, Wolf," I said blandly.

"But what can we do for acclimatization?" he replied in despair.

"Chew rusty nails," I suggested. But the humour was lost on him as he saw his chances of acclimatizing vanish and he nearly became apoplectic. However, chess formed a bond of friendship between us and healed the rift.

WHILE IN KATHMANDU I must have come in contact with an unpleasant virus, and the evening after my return to Base Camp I started coughing and felt very unwell and miserable. I retired to my tent, pitched close by the hospital. My head ached, I felt even more lethargic than usual and sweated profusely. I woke in the night in a terrible panic that something serious had happened to me miles from medical help. I was laid out by an influenza-like illness that caused a raw cough and purulent bronchitis. This would be a minor ailment at home about which one would hardly bother the doctor. But I must stress how different it is to be even mildly ill at 18,000 feet (5,500 metres) and a long way from proper medical facilities. Just being at altitude makes one feel unwell and headaches, pains and irritating little symptoms are all magnified in intensity and cause undue concern to the sufferer. Like athletes preparing for an important race, everyone is keen to be in top physical condition, knowing that a cough or cold at the wrong moment could jeopardize his or her chances on the mountain.

I do not think I am particularly prone to hypochondria but my wife, referring to my letters home on this and previous occasions, has several times commented on my obsession with my state of health and my bowels in particular. Diarrhea can make life extremely unpleasant, causing you to stop for relief in cold inconvenient places on the open mountain and to make long trudges across to the camp latrine at night, sometimes with such urgency that you cannot even reach it in time. The raptures of satisfaction over the passage of a formed stool are difficult to comprehend at home. Being off the food that is so necessary to function efficiently saps strength and morale.

At a height where breath was hard enough to come by I had a rasping cough that racked my chest. A bout of coughing would go on unremittingly for several minutes, leaving me breathless and with aching ribs; it made my throat sore so I could swallow only with discomfort. The lethargy and headache that are part of the illness were added to the habitual lethargy and headache of altitude; my head pounded and all I wanted was to lie still. If I moved from my sleeping bag the change in temperature started another outburst of coughing; at night this completely disrupted sleep that was hard to get anyway because of the altitude.

I lay in my tent without the energy or desire to do anything, just staring at the ridge pole — which was a very boring pole, very straight, shiny and with no rough features to break the monotony of its smooth line. The orange colour of the tent fabric was most unrestful on the eyes and when the sun came out it glared with disturbing brightness.

With the worry of illness came a general feeling of depression and homesickness. I stuck photographs of my family to the lid of my tin trunk which I left open so I could look at them. I wondered what on earth had made me forsake the comfort and security of my home and a family I love for this horrible place. I would have to go up the Icefall in a few days, and this hung over me as a threat to my life.

Sarah was at home with Lucy, who could only say a few words when I left. Would she remember me when I returned? If I did not return she would never really have known me; Adam might, for he was eight and we have done so much together, exploring castles, canoeing, walking round the Snowdon horseshoe. I had many more things planned to do with him when I returned. Was this all worth it for him to be able to say, "My daddy was the doctor on Everest"? Not much good to him really if I did not come back to tell him the story.

When I was kissing Judith goodbye at London airport a big tear rolled off her cheek and she hugged me and said, "You won't fall down that mountain will you, Daddy?" That nearly turned me over and I thought of it on many subsequent occasions and wondered if I had lied when I said, "No, Jo, I'll be back home soon. You look after Mummy and be good."

These morbid thoughts wandered through my mind as my fever rose and I coughed uncontrollably. Ang Tsering brought me tea and a hot water bottle. Being able to listen to cassettes of classical music on my tape recorder helped to pass the time and to sedate my anxieties. The tempest in Beethoven's Pastoral Symphony was sweet compared to the whining of the wind outside and the fury of the afternoon storm.

But the tents were comfortable enough. I had a foam rubber mattress and an inflatable air bed that prevented the cold from rising out of the stony ground. Our sleeping bags were very warm; an inner lightweight down bag fitted into a heavy outer bag with a heavy zip all round. They would have been ideal lashed to a kumatok hauled across the ice by dogs, but when thrust deep into our large pack-frames they were so bulky that little space remained to carry other gear.

One invaluable item of equipment was the plastic urinal. Instead of having to go outside in the cold night air to pass water it could be done in the warmth and comfort of one's own bag. In the morning it was common to see men walking over to the latrines to empty their bottles in the *pissoir*.

I had little urge to read. Sarah's letters were all I could summon the energy for and I gained great pleasure from her accounts of the most mundane details of life at home. Her description of a weekend at our cottage in Wales, the buds coming out and lambs in the fields, enabled me to build a vivid picture of the greenness of pastoral Britain that was so absent on our dull dirty grey moraine.

When I felt better I read *Tess of the D'Urbervilles*; it describes countryside I dearly love and which has so little rival across the world in beauty although it may be less spectacular than some. I have a deep love of Britain and the more widely I travel the more profound it grows. In such a small compass an infinite variety of scenery can be found; history and landscape are intertwined in our heritage of castles, churches and houses; there is a unique subtlety of colour and tone that changes with the seasons.

Travelling abroad is an important part of the education that I would choose for my children, but also it is essential to travel at home and learn to know our island that has so much variety. Then can one overlook the many disadvantages and restrictions of living in Britain and appreciate the privilege of growing up in a country so rich in history. Perhaps present privation was exaggerating my parochialism.

SOON I felt better. Then one morning as I was eating breakfast David Isles sat opposite me coughing hard and looking peculiarly unwell. When he produced a large bolus of yellow sputum I suggested he should come to the hospital. On examining him I discovered that one side of his chest was full of infection and the lower half of the lung was collapsed. I put him to bed in the hospital, letting him breathe a small flow of oxygen to improve his dusky lips, and then I started him on treatment with large doses of an antibiotic. To suffer from pneumonia at that altitude is much more serious than having the same illness at sea level. The reserve capacity of the lung is lower even in health, and when some of that lung is out of action through disease, the remaining lung may not be able to cope with extracting the amount of oxygen that the body needs for normal function.

Having a patient in the hospital was pleasant company for me. David Isles, a mathematics professor at Tufts University, Massachusetts, was endowed with the vague absent-mindedness that is the privilege of his profession. His long hair falls over one eye and he has developed the mannerism of combing it back in place with his fingers and holding his head slightly on one side.

Faced with a problem in geometry his face lights up and his slow drawl audibly quickens. We had tins of Camembert cheese that were opened by winding a key and removing a strip of metal from the middle, leaving two halves of the tin with fairly sharp edges. I posed the question, "Given just the cheese and the circular cutting edge of the tin, how can you divide the cheese into two exactly equal halves?"

This simple problem threw him into mental contortions and he started scribbling on small scraps of paper. Apparently this is a more complicated mathematical concept than I had ever imagined and David promised to set it to his class immediately on return to college in the fall semester.

His climbing had taken him to Peru and Bolivia as well as to many places in the North American continent. He had a pleasant detachment from the intricacies of the expedition and was prepared to go along gently in its wake.

He improved in the hospital on his treatment, but a segment of his lung remained collapsed and as soon as he was mobile I suggested he should go down the valley to convalesce. Eighteen thousand feet (5,500 metres) is no altitude at which to recuperate from pneumonia and a few days lower down, seeing green grass and flowers again, would restore his morale and allow him to eat fresh food.

CHAPTER 9

During the time when the Icefall route was being prospected, the leaders had remained at Base Camp overseeing the onward movement towards the foot of the mountain.

Two more different men could hardly be imagined than Norman Dyhrenfurth and Jimmy Roberts and yet they were complementary to each other. Their respective jobs were so different that they seldom came into conflict. Norman dealt with the executive problems, finance and overall control of the climbers; Jimmy organized the Sherpas and all the logistics of moving our stores and equipment up to Advance Base Camp.

Norman had led the formidable American Mount Everest expedition in 1963, when the mountain was climbed on two different occasions by the South Col and also by a West Ridge route which included a digression onto the Northwest Face by Unsoeld and Hornbein — two Americans treading the ground of the Tibetan People's Communist Republic. The members were not particularly experienced outside America, there were no really "hard" men and no one had climbed in the Himalayas before.

Norman had spent two years preparing, and a similar length of time paying off the bills and tidying up after the expedition, and even then he got landed with a lot of acrimony and gained little credit for leading what must be counted as one of the most successful expeditions of modern times. Few people appreciate that Norman climbed to over 28,000 feet (8,500 metres), filming in place of the professional cameraman, who had fallen sick, and supporting the summit teams.

It is hard to understand how he was prepared to let himself in for all this labour again, armed with the knowledge that it might end up for him personally in the same sad way and need even more hard work. As he said himself, "The public have lost interest in Everest; now they are even blasé about the moon."

For at least two years Norman worked full-time organizing our expedition, typing all his own letters without the help of a secretary and chasing unwilling donors of money to the distant corners of the world, which involved him in countless complicated business ventures in order to raise the $200,000 needed to have the expedition equipped, provisioned and transported to Mount Everest. He sent regular and detailed circular letters to team members, who changed with remarkable frequency in the early days, and kept in touch with them all closely by personal mail.

Jimmy Roberts could not have been more of a contrast yet he and Norman managed to get on remarkably well without treading on each other's toes. Each knew his own job, respected the other's and tried hard not to interfere.

Jimmy is shy to a point of brusqueness and predictably British in his sense of humour and his under-dramatization of crises. His understanding of the Sherpas is unique; he has spent his lifetime with Gurkhas, he speaks their language and they respect his authority and scrupulous fairness and they like him, for they know exactly where they stand; no nonsense, no idling, no humbug. He used to limp round camp on his arthritic hip, which has become more painful and stiff in recent years following an old injury and the strain put on it by many hundreds of miles tramping the mountains of Nepal, grunting commands and organizing the men. Then he would return to his tent where his belongings were laid out in orderly array; binoculars, a copy of *Sporting Life*, a book on birds and many old copies of the *Hindustan Times*, a bottle of whisky and his urine flask. Usually a young helper was hovering close by awaiting orders and ready to jump at his bark, which got things done quicker than anyone else could. Often Jimmy would not appear from his tent for meals, preferring to eat on his own, but when he was in the mess tent and feeling relaxed he was entertaining company.

Jimmy originally had every intention of climbing through the Icefall to Camp II, and certainly his hip would not have prevented him as it had not hindered him on the 200-mile (320-kilometre) march-in. But the complicated administration at Base Camp required his presence there continually. His job was one demanding experience and knowledge of the country. He scribbled his calculations of loads and manpower on loose sheets of paper in the form of a military plan of action, and the veritable mountain of equipment found its way up the Icefall in a way that never ceased to cause me wonder. To sit at Base Camp for a couple of months directing the action yet unable to take part in it required consid-erable moral stamina and Jimmy's attitude of mind was equal to it. I used to be scared of him, but as I broke through the barrier of his remoteness we became friends — never close, but I was conscious of mutual esteem though he couched any appreciation he had of the medical services in terms of cynicism that I took for affection.

I STILL HAD much work to do to complete the medical packs before I went up the mountain. I wanted to make sure that at no time was a member of the expedition far from medicines that he might need. So I set about organizing it in the following manner.

Each man would carry with him all the time a small individual pack which fitted into an air-sealed plastic box four inches (ten centimetres) square by two inches (five centimetres) deep. It contained a few Elastoplast dressings, a bandage, some antiseptic ointment and cream to prevent

sunburn and, wrapped in self-sealing plastic envelopes, a few pills for
sore throat, headache, sleeping and diarrhea. Each envelope was carefully
labelled: for example, "Ronicol for frostbite," "Amethocaine drops for
snowblindness."

This individual box would allow a climber to start sufficient elemen-
tary treatment to last him until he could reach a camp. Each camp on
both the Face and the Ridge had a more elaborate medical box in a
similar type of plastic container but three times as large. It held a bigger
selection of bandages and dressings, and the drugs included morphia
(marked "on doctor's orders only"), purple-heart dexedrine capsules
(marked "only to be used in descent to aid reaching camp") and a powerful antibiotic with a wide range of action. The idea was that once a patient
had arrived at a camp he could be instructed over the radio on what treatment he should start until one of the doctors could reach him. A space
blanket was included in the Camp Box so that someone who needed to
be carried or lowered down the mountain could be wrapped in this large
sheet of silver foil, which would enable him to conserve his body heat.

Two doctors' "High Boxes" held a full range of emergency medical
equipment including inflatable splints, plaster of Paris and the more
powerful drugs. In a separate case was a resuscitation set like a small
anaesthetic outfit; it contained a self-expanding bellows that could be
used to breathe for an unconscious patient through a tube passed via the
mouth into the lungs, and all the emergency vials for giving drugs into
a vein were stored in little compartmented plastic boxes.

With these two boxes David Peterson or I could set off up the mountain to administer first aid to someone in trouble before bringing them
down to Advance Base or Base Camp, where we had tin trunks full of
medicines, dressings and surgical equipment.

On April 7 Carlo Mauri came down to Base Camp with prolapsed
piles, a condition of altitude as common as it is uncomfortable. I began
to suffer shortly afterwards and a total of five expedition members had to
be treated for this problem. I think it must result from carrying heavy
loads and overbreathing, both of which combine to increase the pressure

inside the abdomen and coincidentally raise the pressure of the veins in the back passage, which become dilated at their weak points. On Annapurna the previous year Dougal Haston bled so heavily from piles that he was forced to wear a towel for a week, but this bad attack must have clotted the veins completely and cured his condition so he had no further trouble on Everest this year.

Carlo Mauri was very depressed with his uncomfortable bottom and was worried lest it would interfere with his chances on the mountain. He was also being troubled by an old skiing injury to his leg that had once put him in hospital for three years because of complications that set in and left him with a permanent limp. On top of these physical woes Carlo had found, on the glacier of the Western Cwm, the remains of a body that had been tied up in a rope and put into a crevasse, but with the movement of the glacier had come to the surface several years after being buried. Norman Dyhrenfurth thought it must have been the body of Sherpa Mingma Dorji, who was killed by falling ice in 1955 on the Swiss Lhotse expedition. Episodes like this make even the most hardened mountaineer think deeply, and the experience obviously troubled Carlo.

We had a long talk in the hospital, Carlo lying out on my bed, I sitting at my desk. We had become close friends since our arrival in Kathmandu, when I had done a lot of exploring and guiding with him and the Vauchers on our bicycle rides round lesser-known parts of the valley. *Caro dottore*, he used to call me, "dear doctor," and I think he really meant it. We talked of his home town, Lecco, and his valley, which lies in the central Italian Alps at the point where Italy, Switzerland and Austria meet, and he told me a little of his family, a subject he did not often mention. "I have spent so much of my life away on seventeen different expeditions that I find I cannot stay at home for more than a few months," he told me. "I get too restless."

Carlo Mauri is a household name in Italy, where he is a legendary adventurer. He began as a ski and mountain guide, doing many hard first ascents in the Alps with his friend Walter Bonatti. His first visit to the Himalayas was on an expedition led by Fosco Maraini to Masherbrum in the Karakoram range and later he went to the Hindu Kush in Afghanistan.

He has been on ten expeditions to the South American Andes. Not all his exploration has been in mountains. His travels have taken him to Spitsbergen in the Arctic, to Antarctica, to New Zealand and New Guinea and across the Atlantic with Thor Heyerdal on the raft *Ra*.

His usual bonhomie was subdued as we talked in the hospital and he became morose as he described the Icefall. "*Il est très dangereux,*" he said repeatedly, and with his big bushy beard he looked like a sad lion rather than the proud beast with the majestic mane that I knew before.

But as he improved with treatment his old good humour returned and we made plans to go up to Camp II together after a few days.

Pierre Mazeaud had also come down vociferously deploring the terrible food at Advance Base Camp and bemoaning the lack of fresh meat. He was trained in law as a magistrate and is now a deputy of the French National Assembly, representing a suburb of Paris as a member of Parliament. Of slight build and sharp feature, Pierre was a firm follower of *le Général*, Charles de Gaulle. He was the first Frenchman on Everest and made no secret of how important this was for the Republic and for himself.

His command of language and rhetoric was impressive and, as the newspapers arrived with the mail runner, we could tell that some new election was afoot and the results were soon obvious by the barometric appearance on Pierre's face. He had the dash of the politician in his speech and expansive hand gestures to go with it. His climbing experience had been limited to the Alps, where he had accumulated a fine record of difficult ascents; one in particular being notable for his surviving a series of disasters on the central pillar of Freney, where several people lost their lives during eleven days spent on the mountain.

Like a true Frenchman, his ultimate desire at Base Camp was for *une bouteille de vin très ordinaire et un bifteck* ("a bottle of very ordinary wine and a steak"). He had reason to complain about the food. To choose a diet that would satisfy the extremes of taste, from porridge and haggis eaters on one hand to those who delight in suki-yaki and seaweed or smorgasbord on the other, was almost impossible. The food we had to eat was not only dehydrated or from tins, but of a monotony that only an ardent

European black bread and black sausage enthusiast could stomach. My complaint, voiced soon after arrival at Base Camp, was not against the individual foods, but because so little fresh food was being bought.

We ate powdered sauté mash in a land where the potato is king and can be bought by the sackload. (Warren Hastings, when governor of Bengal for the East India Company, ordered his officers going into the Himalayas on political missions to plant seed potatoes at every camping stop.) Pumpernickel, Knäckebrot and Zwieback were our bread substitutes when flour and ground maize could be bought locally and baked by our excellent cook, Danu. Tasty yak butter is made in Khumbu; the Swiss dairies at Giri and in the Langtang also produce first-class cheese; instead we had a synthetic substitute for butter, Camembert in tins and Cheddar slivers wrapped in plastic packets.

Delicacies were plentiful: herrings in rich white sauce, seven-inch-long wieners, pickled gherkins and beetroot, shredded celery in mayonnaise, pork pâté in tubes. To the sea level stomach these sound appetizing, but high-up tastes change and however glossy the label on the tin its contents pall rapidly. We all longed for fresh food; no amount of Biostrath (much sought after by the Sherpas for its fifteen percent alcohol content rather than its vitamins), Biomaltz, Vitalzin or Complan with all their nutritional supplements can keep an expedition fit as fresh food will.

To keep a group of people taking heavy physical exercise in peak fitness, fresh food must be acquired at any price. Sheep and goats can be bought on the hoof in Khumbu at reasonable price; they could even be marched in with the expedition, carrying panniers on their backs, and slaughtered as needed. The meat could be cooked at Base Camp on wood fires and sent up to the higher camps to be rewarmed; Spam in every stew soon becomes unpalatable. Fresh vegetables are grown in Kathmandu and in May cabbage, cauliflower and carrots were flown to Lukla in time for us to eat as we were leaving. Dehydrated soups, peas and sundry other vegetables swelled in the stomach and gave a false illusion of satiety, but they produced an astonishing volume of gas with foul odour that was a persistent, anti-social problem. Passage of flatus in company is an unforgivable breach of manners to the Sherpa; to many members it caused loud mirth, to others gross irritation.

But we had plenty of fresh eggs that were brought up packed in boxes with moss and these were always appreciated. I am well aware that for an expedition the size of a small army it is not possible to live entirely off the land. However, I had visited the weekly market at Namche Bazaar where men come from as far as Okhaldhunga and Aisyalukharka five days to the south in order to sell their produce. In large sacks they bring rice, which is the most compact staple cereal; and dal or lentils, which has the highest protein content of any vegetable.

On previous Himalayan journeys I had lived almost entirely on local food; with a hundred mouths to feed it is a different matter, but much can be bought and though the price may be high it is doubtful whether it would compare with the cost of equivalent items brought from Europe, albeit freely donated.

We had sufficient to drink. Twelve hundred cans of beer were carried in, weighing the same as all my medical supplies put together. There was whisky for the sahibs and rum for the Sherpas — and much else besides. The Sherpas' womenfolk kept a steady supply of rakshi, a home-brewed spirit, flowing up the Khumbu moraine and down the gullets of their men, some of whom would be quite comatose soon after a new consignment arrived, and ribald laughing by the remaining sober ones would go on late into the night.

But Danu did his best to give us good meals and Carlo taught him to make a pasta from noodles, tuna fish and tomato sauce from tubes.

Danu is a Sherpa gentleman, always impeccably polite, a short, solid man with a quaint mannerism of folding his arms, with one hand, index finger extended, held pensively against his cheek.

I first met him at Jomossom in 1962 when he was cook to the Dutch Nilgiri expedition that had descended the same evening as I arrived, from the opposite direction. He cooked a celebration feast to which I was invited and I had the pleasure of sitting beside Lionel Terray, who in that one season had climbed Jannu in the Kanchenjunga massif before the monsoon, the south face of Aconcagua in Peru while rain was falling on the Himalayas, and returned to Nepal in the autumn to help the Dutch reach the top of Nilgiri. At that feast (I had eaten little more than maize and potatoes for the previous month) I heard a selection of English lyrics richer than I had learnt from any of my loud-mouthed rugger friends at university.

The weather at our camp was very poor in the afternoons and snow would sometimes fall heavily so that a dusty white pall covered the ground and the orange tents stuck out, looking ghostly in the dull overcast of low cloud. Coldness seeped into the air early and I was glad to put on my heavy down clothing by three o'clock.

One afternoon, when the sun broke through and showed the peaks at the bottom of the valley clear and beautiful, I took Murray Sayle out onto the glacier to try out his crampons. We had an entertaining walk through some ice corridors and across small frozen lakes under which we could hear water tearing down to meet the river. We came across a camp of several years before with some old oxygen bottles and bamboo marker flags and even an unopened tin of cheese that we guessed must have belonged to the Swiss in 1952.

This was Murray's first time on crampons and considering his totally unathletic physique he made a good effort, after a few altercations over his technique had taken place. Just being out of sight of Base Camp was a pleasure and some of the ice pinnacles and the icicles that hung from them were beautiful indeed.

Back at camp that evening, as we were sitting in the mess tent waiting for the kitchen workers to bring the soup, the cry went up, "*Dak walla ayo*: the mail runner has come."

I forgot the soup and ran outside, clambering onto the nearest boulder to gain a better view down the moraine path. Several hundred yards off two figures were approaching at a trot and I could see Gyaltsen and Ang Hritta, Sherpa mail carriers, hurrying along the rock-strewn way.

The mail was distributed; as with exam results, the names of those who have passed are called out and you wait in anxious expectancy. I had a letter from Sarah full of all the sort of things I wanted to hear about:

We are all very well and went to the cottage at Blaenau at the weekend. It was a beautiful day, warm and sunny. We walked up to the pipe across the river by the tumble-down stone pen and the kids had a marvellous time walking across the pipe, at least Adam walked and Judith inched a little way across on her bottom. We then explored up the hill behind the house and down to the stream, the buds were beginning to come out on the trees and there are some wild daffodils in the garden. Lucy and I picnicked on the grass outside the house — they had a marvellous time pulling down the old chicken house and made a lovely den for themselves and built a little fireplace where Adam cooked his fried eggs. On Sunday it was back to typical Welsh drizzle, but it didn't seem to matter and we explored below the house where the two rivers meet.

This particular evening, not only did they bring the mail but some chickens as well. This was a thrill indeed and we decided to postpone the soup indefinitely to allow Danu to prepare them — our first fresh meat for several weeks. To fill the intervening minutes and in celebration of this happy event, Jimmy Roberts ordered a couple of bottles of whisky to be opened. They helped to oil us up, ready to battle with the chickens, which must have done a great deal of mountaineering in their day judging by the toughness of the meat.

CHAPTER 10

On the morning of April 14 I left with Carlo Mauri and Pierre Mazeaud to climb through the Icefall to Camp I. The morning was clear although small puffs of cloud hung over the Western Shoulder heralding an early disappearance of the sun, a weather pattern to which we were now accustomed. We put on crampons very soon when the rock of the moraine gave way to glacier ice and, using ski sticks for balance, we went unroped. Pierre Mazeaud struck off ahead; I followed in the steps of Carlo, who set a steady pace. The first part of the climb was easy, not steep, and I found it pleasant in the crisp morning air. We were still in shadow and surrounded by tall pinnacled ice seracs and crevasses as yet a safe way off.

I had dreaded this day all the previous year and thinking about the Icefall had caused me nightmares. About to embark on it for the first time, I felt just as I do when I sit in my canoe on a river and the water ahead is smooth as it spills over the lip of a fall and I can't yet see the white water, I just hear it, and then all of a sudden I'm in the rapid with water coming from every direction, roar, chaos, action and fighting to stay upright.

I hadn't slept much the previous night and breakfast lay heavy on my stomach as nausea welled up inside. But I now felt committed and the fear was a little subdued by knowing that I was being accompanied by Carlo Mauri, one of the most experienced of all Italian guides.

The route winds through the Icefall like a big letter "S," starting from the bottom left-hand corner and finally disappearing at the last big wall which guards the entrance to the Cwm 2,000 feet (600 metres) higher. Bridges made of two logs placed beside each other had been built across the small crevasses in the lower part. Bamboo sticks carrying red flags acted as markers to show the path and remained visible even after a heavy snowfall. Our way wound in and out of small seracs, which are towers of ice left after a section of wall becomes detached from the main body of the moving glacier.

After climbing for an hour we stopped for a rest at Dump Camp. This had been used as a cache for material when the Icefall route was being pioneered. I was finding no problem with the altitude, mainly because Carlo's pace was so measured and gentle. Carlo sat on his rucksack, bronzed, bearded, relaxed in an environment that is his own; but again he said, "It's very dangerous."

So far I had been surprised by the ease of the climb. We were now almost level with the Lho La and could peer over it into Tibet. On the other side lies the Rongbuk glacier, gateway to a thousand mysterious places the names of which evoke exciting and romantic pictures — Shigatse, Gyantse, Lhasa — the whole of that vast forbidden upland plateau of the Trans-Himalaya. We set off from Dump Camp and entered the most contorted part of the Icefall. The area was chaotically shattered — a scene of confusion on a scale of fearsome immensity, totally lacking in order or pattern. Blocks weighing many tons had to be skirted and the passages and crevasses between them were deep and dark. When I had time to look around I saw a place of unique beauty with fantastic carved patterns strangely contrasting with the elegant shapes of the surrounding mountains.

Aluminium ladders had been set up to scale short vertical walls that could not be climbed by heavily laden Sherpas. They were secured in place by two-foot-long (60-centimetre) metal stakes hammered deep to their hilt in the snow, so giving a firm belay for attaching the top of the ladder. Care was needed in placing our feet in order to avoid catching the long metal spikes of our crampons on a rung of the ladder. The crevasses in this section were much wider and were bridged either by logs or by aluminium ladders laid horizontally. A rope handrail, that provided reassurance more moral than real, was put up when the gap was more than six feet (two metres) wide. Any weight put onto it caused the rope to give outwards and one's body would sway over space. The blue-green colour in the depths of a chasm gets darker the deeper it goes and glistening vertical walls of ice beckon seductively. I felt sympathy for the terror that Jonah must have entertained as he gazed into the gaping jaws of the whale and saw the dark confines of its belly close at hand. Even more care was needed on the horizontal ladders, for the crampons collected a ball of compacted snow between the spikes and became slippery on the metal ladder rungs, tending to roll forwards out of control. Ski sticks afforded some balance and halfway across one could lean forwards and plant them in the snow on the far side. In all there were more than 30 different bridges or ladders to cross.

We rounded a corner overhung by a small serac and climbed down a steep snow slide with the help of a fixed rope — a section of rope attached to pitons firmly driven into the ice to use as a handrail. Ahead lay the "mane wall," 100 yards (91 metres) long, 60 feet (18 metres) high and weighing 30,000 tons, overhanging the gully up which we had to climb.

High up on the "mane wall" a section of wire ladder from the previous year's Japanese expedition hung free at an angle of 30 degrees from the face, emphasizing the overhang and showing how radically the Icefall changes in the course of time. Bamboo poles could be seen standing on isolated pinnacles away off in the distance, separated from us by a tangled white mass. I said a prayer myself as we started up the passage and climbed as quickly as we could. But to hurry at this height is useless as you soon become breathless and exhausted and have to stop for rest. A certain detachment of mind is required to plod slowly up a place as dangerous as this. On the ground lay the debris of snow and ice from a large section of the wall that had collapsed four days previously a few minutes after a group of Sherpas had passed by on their way up to Camp I. The blocks were of a size that would have pulverized anyone underneath them when they fell. We heard a continuous creaking and groaning as the depths of the Icefall broke up in its relentless onward and downward movement.

Once beyond the shadow of the wall and on safe ground again, we looked back. Only from above could we see the gash a hundred feet (thirty metres) deep that separated the "mane wall" from the main body of the glacier, so that it leant over, teetering, unstable and liable to collapse any time — as indeed it did, piece by piece in the following days. By incredible fortune this happened usually at night, and each time we reassured ourselves that the route had become just a little bit safer, but all things in the Icefall are relative. Near here in 1963, Jake Breitenbach, one of the strongest young climbers of the American Everest expedition, had been killed by a falling wall of ice. Ang Pema had been close beside but he narrowly escaped, though his face was badly cut. Despite this awful experience Ang Pema had returned to Everest with us and had gone up the Icefall again to be cook at Advance Base.

After another half-hour we came to the final problem that lay below the wall forming the lip of the Western Cwm. The geography was quite distorted and looked as though a large area had sunk into the mountain, leaving a wide crevasse. This was bridged by a section of aluminium ladder joined to a wire caving ladder with short rungs that swung loosely over the abyss. We passed a group of roped Sherpas running down after depositing their heavy loads at Camp I. They danced confidently across these hazards and their exuberance filled me with admiration and forbade any show of fear I might have felt.

Beyond the bridge we climbed a corner and stepped into a gallery about twenty feet (six metres) long leading to the foot of a ladder that mounted the last vertical wall. At the top Carlo and I began coughing uncontrollably, causing us to vomit; our stomachs only had orange juice to work on and the ensuing cramps were painful. I do not know why this suddenly attacked us, as till then we had suffered no effects of altitude.

We now entered the Western Cwm and the terrain became smoother; but where the glacier was beginning to break away, deep long crevasses were formed, stretching from one enclosing wall to the other like bacon falling fresh-cut off a slicer. This year sufficient natural snow bridges remained so that in order to avoid crevasses we could make a zig-zag track. Marker flags led us on towards Camp I, where we found Pierre Mazeaud brewing tea. Clouds had rolled up the valley and snow began to fall; soon thunder broke and boomed across from the face of Nuptse to the west, reverberating round the Cwm and breaking the eerie stillness.

Camp I at 20,300 feet (6,200 metres) had half a dozen orange tents pitched on a sloping snow field twenty yards (eighteen metres) across with deep chasms on either side — no place for a sleepwalker. Much equipment had now been accumulated in the big lift of the past few days and was waiting to be carried on to Advance Base at the far end of the Cwm.

Bill Kurban's genial voice greeted me, "I think you'd better go and see Pin Howell; he's pretty sick. He's hardly left his tent for two days."

I found Pin in his sleeping bag looking a ghastly colour. "I couldn't sleep when I arrived here so I took some of those pills you gave me."

"Some. How many's that?" I asked.

"Oh, only five. Do you think that's too many?"

"Only five times the normal dose, you idiot! I'm surprised you ever woke up," I said. He was vomiting and feeling awful. "I expect you'll take a few days to sleep it off, then when you're better come on up to II. I'm going on tomorrow with Carlo."

His lips were very cracked and his tongue had developed deep sore fissures, so in a small tube I made up a solution from gentian violet crystals. With his white face and purple-painted mouth he looked like a circus clown.

After the luxuries of Base Camp, life at Camp I appeared primitive. We now had to cook on temperamental paraffin stoves and every drop of water had to be melted from snow; no longer were there firewood and running water. The cooking tent was small and uncomfortable with no proper place to sit; we crouched, trying to keep dry by avoiding the pools of water that were accumulating on the floor. Gary Colliver appeared and welcomed us. He had come up a day or so earlier and was still coughing harshly.

Gary is American but for some while he has been working in a biology laboratory in Canada as a research assistant. He lives in Calgary on the prairie at the foot of the Rockies with easy access to the big mountains. He made his name as a rock climber in California's Yosemite Valley, where he has done many hard routes including the gigantic precipice on the Nose of El Capitan. He has also been on expeditions to Peru and to Mount McKinley in Alaska; this was his first visit to the Himalayas. Of medium height, bespectacled and bearded, Gary is a friendly companion and a formidable worker.

While we were drinking tea and Carlo was preparing an Italian pasta from some spaghetti and tins of meat with tomato sauce out of toothpaste tubes, shouts of the Sherpas arriving from Camp II broke the quiet.

I was warmly greeted by Pemba Thondup Kunde, a strong, wild-looking young Sherpa.

"How's your arm?" I asked him.

"Better, sir, thank you. No more trouble with bootlaces," he replied in Nepali. Before we left Kathmandu he had been fooling around learning to ride a bicycle in the courtyard of the hotel and had fallen off and injured his elbow. I took him for an x-ray and, on finding a small fracture, put him in a clean new plaster of Paris splint. While walking back through the middle of the town he tripped over his untied bootlaces in the main street and fell forwards. He put his arm out to break his fall, cracked the new plaster and nearly fractured his arm again. All he could do was laugh when I rounded on him for his ineptitude, but he was grateful for my attention and we became good friends. Ang Nima Phortse had also arrived, a round-faced cherubic lad, who assured me that his worms had disappeared now after two strong doses of medicine.

Carlo and I retired to our tent early and talked. He told me about the Ra expedition that he had just been on. It also was an international party —a Norwegian, a Russian, an American, an Arab, a Mexican, a man from Chad and an Italian, and all had worked together in perfect amity.

"I like the sea, you just lie there and the wind and the currents help you along, and it is warm and there's nothing to do but think. I like the sea in Italy too and the girls there are pretty." He extolled the virtues of *giovanni fanciulle* ("young lasses") and we thought about them for a while, but soon the conversation changed to food and our expedition. "For me Everest is very important," said Carlo.

As there was nothing to stay up for we got into our bags and settled down to sleep while the wind outside moaned quietly. The following morning was clear and we set off up the Cwm, Pierre Mazeaud again forging ahead, a lone figure in a vast white expanse. The crevasses beyond Camp I were wider than any we had crossed so far and the bridges more spectacular. Gradually the track swung towards the face of Nuptse and passed under the wall that rose for several thousand feet of glistening slabs, down which snow and ice fell at intervals. Crossing such an avalanche line was precarious, as we could judge from the debris lying around our track. The fine snow powder that is thrown up during an avalanche is as dangerous as the ice blocks themselves, for it gets deep down in the lungs and suffocates. We moved as fast as we could from this place and soon regained the safety of the centre of the Cwm.

This enormous ice field, walled in on all sides, rose gradually towards the Lhotse face, the end barrier to the valley. The sun shone, the air was still, all was quiet. Aptly called by the Swiss the Valley of Silence, this name is much more descriptive of the place than the Western "Cwm," a Welsh word given to it by George Mallory out of enthusiasm for his native rock climbing ground. Hunt refers to it as a high-level glen. What a pity we transpose parochial terms applicable to our own hills to these mountains which have their own far more suitable and beautiful Sherpa or

Tibetan names. The English name of Everest itself is a sad choice; it is called after a retired imperial surveyor-general, Sir George Everest, who had not even seen it. What more beautiful name could there be than "Chomolungma," and what more beautiful and applicable meaning than "Goddess-mother of the world"?

The sun beat down on the snow, which reflected unfiltered ultraviolet rays that burnt the undersides of our nostrils and our lips. Carlo's bushy beard protected much of his face; mine by contrast was thin and under-nourished, with bald patches in need of a good fertilizer. Nevertheless, not having to shave was a lazy pleasure. We were stripped to our shirt sleeves so had to take care not to expose too much of our skin to the vicious sun. Goggles or dark glasses are essential protection to avoid burning the cornea, or window of the eye, which results in snowblindness. At Base Camp I had instructed the Sherpas how to make a simple protective shield from a piece of cardboard and string. I had learnt the trick from the Labrador Inuit, who cut one-inch horizontal slits in a piece of wood hollowed out to fit snugly round the eyes and secured it round the head with a thong. Cutting similar slits in a piece of shaped cardboard or paper is ample first aid for a climber who has dropped or broken his sunglasses.

Despite this precaution three Sherpas later suffered from snowblindness. The burn breaks the thin epithelial covering of the cornea, exposing many sensitive nerve endings, and causes exquisite pain, especially in bright light. The eyes water and the lids and conjunctiva swell up, closing the eye tight, which gives the condition the erroneous name of "blindness." With adequate treatment the cornea will heal in a few days but the person is completely useless during this time. A small dropper containing local anaesthetic was included in every individual and camp medical box. This would be sufficient to remove the searing pain from a burnt eye and allow the climber to return under his own power to a camp, but it would play no part in the healing. A "blind" man on a mountain is a great hazard to himself and his companions and prevention is a serious matter.

The Face of Mount Everest suddenly stood before us to the left of the head of the Cwm. This 7,000-foot-high (2,100-metre) pyramid of black rock dusted with snow had remained hidden from view until this minute. Below Namche we had caught our first glimpse of the final thousand feet (three hundred metres) of the summit cone peering over the massive deadpan wall of Nuptse that intervened between us. Even beyond Thyangboche the summit was still visible, but became smaller as we approached Pheriche. Then it disappeared, not to be seen again until this dramatic moment.

How did I feel then, face to face with the highest mountain in the world? I was overawed; not by its beauty, for I do not consider it beautiful, but by its size, by its sinister blackness, by its history. Everest has become a legend to many people the world over. Climbers have assaulted it for fifty years with many failures and some successes; they have been disappointed on it, maimed on it, died on it, and yet the legend still has the power to draw them back again.

From where we stood we could see the top and the plume of snow being blown off it by the vicious winds that form a vortex over the summit cone. The Face is foreshortened from such proximity and appears to lean backwards, so making the steepness of it less than in reality. But its sheer size was commanding, oppressive, ugly, mysterious. A host of undecipherable emotions swept over me and I felt that I had met the tiger who would have me quick as a flash if I placed a foot wrong, whose eyes glinted at me as the sun did off the icy patches on the mountain.

Certain features stood out: the sweeping central buttress and ice contour that soared up the Face, dividing into a Y whose two arms embraced the wall and the yellow band above. Otherwise the Face was plain, very steep, very unwelcoming.

Carlo and I sat down to rest below Camp II, which was yet hidden beyond a rim of snow. We saw a figure approaching; it was Antony Thomas descending alone to Camp I.

"That last rise is never-ending. I don't know why because it's not far to camp," he said. "You'll be there in twenty minutes, but it's an awful slog."

After our gentle rise up the Cwm the inclination took the wind out of us and when we eventually crested the ridge we were overjoyed to see the tents of Camp II.

I was pleased to meet so many companions again, some of whom I had not seen since I had left for Kathmandu with the Spaniard two weeks before. Norman Dyhrenfurth and Duane Blume had arrived the day before. Dougal Haston and Don Whillans had just come down from the Face after several days working to put up Camp III. Dougal immediately set off down to Base Camp to rest while Don, being of a more indolent nature, decided to sit where he was. Odd Eliassen had been carrying loads on the West Ridge with Jon Teigland, who followed Dougal down. Toni Hiebeler had made one journey towards Camp III on the Face but was very sick with the altitude and was now lying in his tent feeling unwell and complaining of lack of sleep. He had been ill all the march-in and was now obviously in no shape to go high on the mountain.

I think of Toni Hiebeler in the mess tent, a jovial extrovert holding the company at supper in convulsions of mirth. He sports a thick beard and short-cropped hair with a boyish fringe and he was one of the father figures of the expedition. He is editor of *Alpinismus*, a popular mountaineering journal, and has a distinguished climbing record in the Alps. He was the first man to climb the Eiger Nordwand in winter and has been on expeditions to Mount Elbruz in the Russian Caucasus and Mount Lenin in the Russian Pamirs but never to the Himalayas.

Toni spoke no other language but his own and showed little intention of wanting to learn. I do not know if his Bavarian heritage accounts for his particular brand of humour, but listening to one of Toni's long jokes, at which he himself laughed convulsively, it was exceptional not to hear the words *toiletten-papier* or *scheisse* spoken. We talked to him in a strange mixture of languages and he always smiled and was friendly, but if things became incomprehensible and the excitement of the discussion got out of hand one just shouted "*bahnhof!*" in a guttural, Teutonic voice and he would collapse laughing.

Toni was never well. He caught a bug in Kathmandu that gave him diarrhea and despite our attempts at treatment, which would succeed for a day or two, the trouble inevitably returned and made his march a miserable dash from one bush to another. He lost a lot of weight and arrived not in prime condition at Base Camp, where he had problems in acclimatizing to the altitude. He was a soft-hearted, deeply religious man and became, even more than most of us, very homesick for his wife, to whom he wrote long letters daily. He was a sympathetic man and his clownish humour was a pleasure to experience; we all liked Toni.

When I suggested he might be wise to descend to Base Camp he accepted the idea with alacrity and set off down the Cwm with Leo Schlömmer, who had himself been troubled with insomnia. Wolfgang Axt and Harsh Bahuguna were pushing up towards Camp III on the West Ridge and we could see them on a snow field above through binoculars. Juréc Surdel came down from Camp III West and he too went on down to Base for a rest. John Evans and John Cleare were sharing a tent together; both were going strongly. The Japanese pair, Naomi Uemura and Reizo Ito, were going up to replace the Britons on the Face. Yvette and Michel Vaucher were at Camp II and gave me their usual warm welcome.

The feeling was one of dynamism; everyone was active, things were moving on the mountain and the place hummed with busyness. The weather was clear in the mornings and the sun shone, beating down into the Western Cwm, which sweltered like a furnace. About midday the clouds closed in and snow flurries fell as the weather began to deteriorate, the winds rose, the temperature fell and a storm was upon us.

The following day was fine and in the clear morning air, through Norman Dyhrenfurth's powerful binoculars, I could see the two small figures of Wolfgang Axt and Harsh Bahuguna, one above the other, climbing roped up the steep snow slope towards the Western Shoulder. Three days before they had pitched Camp III well along the face at the end of a line of crevasses at a height of 23,500 feet (7,200 metres). Odd Eliassen and Jon Teigland spent a few days exploring two ice gullies that led straight up to the West Ridge from Camp III. They had the idea of climbing one of these gullies, fixing winches on the ridge and thus hauling up a lot of gear. This route could have avoided the long traverse left onto the Western Shoulder and also a long section of the lower part of the ridge, but unfortunately it had proved impracticable because of the steep snow which was in danger of avalanching and the rock that fell continually into the gully.

Camp III on the Face was already placed at 23,000 feet (7,000 metres) in the lee of a rock buttress at the top of a thousand-foot (three-hundred-metre) snow slope that was festooned with fixed ropes up which the Sherpas could climb quickly. They were using jumars, small devices which can be clipped onto the rope, with a ratchet that allows them to slide up the rope but will jam tight when a downward pull is exerted on them. Don Whillans and Dougal Haston were the first occupants of Camp III. John Evans, Leo Schlömmer and the two Japanese had helped to carry equipment up. On the metal frames left behind by the Japanese expedition they placed a tent and a Whillans "box." The "box" is an oblong, pole-framed shelter designed by Don which has the advantage of being stronger and more stable than the conventional tent, having more space inside. Snow collects on its flat roof and melts in the sunshine which provides drinking water and saves valuable fuel.

Despite all our setbacks the attack on the mountain had really begun in earnest. On the 16th Don Whillans and Dougal Haston came down from the Face for a rest as they had been in the front of the hard work since the first foray into the Icefall and had remained there ever since. Their place was taken by Naomi Uemura and Reizo Ito. Dougal, Jon Teigland and Leo Schlömmer sensibly decided that they would have more rest and nourishment by descending all the way to Base Camp and set off later in the day.

Men were coming and going in different directions and the atmosphere was exciting. I went to bed in a larger tent than I was accustomed to, which felt very spacious. I moved the only medical box that had arrived into the tent, which was to be used as a hospital for Advance Base Camp. In the urgency of lifting oxygen, food and climbing materials up to the foot of the mountain, the medical equipment had taken a low place in the order of priorities. Now that so many men were active on the mountain and continually exposed to danger, I felt strongly that we must have adequate medical stores up there to deal with an emergency that could happen at any time. I could understand that my pleas went unanswered; each person considered the loads that were his special interest to be of prime importance, and the number of loads that could be carried in a day was limited.

April 17 was fine again and Norman Dyhrenfurth talked with the men on the mountain, keeping a controlling hand on the overall plan yet allowing as much latitude as possible to the coordinators of the two teams. He preferred not to interfere with their decisions but to watch developments diplomatically from close at hand, a policy for which he was subsequently severely criticized. That day he advised Wolfgang Axt and Harsh Bahuguna to come down for a break as they had been working hard on the Ridge route for the previous five days. But they asked to stay for an extra day or so as they were so close to finding a site for Camp IV West.

Michel Vaucher and Odd Eliassen went up to straighten out the route to Camp III. At that time a long descent was made before climbing up the last stretch to the camp; at the end of a long carry it was exhausting and an unnecessary waste of effort. They climbed round a steep ice corner and across a snow couloir, placing 350 feet (106 metres) of fixed ropes. The first 40 yards (36 metres) was not exceptionally difficult ground and the corner was the only part requiring alpine skill. They cut steps in all the steeper places and hammered in ice pitons with carabiner snap links at intervals of 10 yards (nine metres). The final 80 yards (73 metres) after the stance in the couloir was a walk on gentle-angled snow.

On the same day Carlo Mauri and Pierre Mazeaud left Advance Base to carry loads up to Camp III West. Pierre claimed his sack weighed as much as a full climbing load but, while he was engaged in the discussion, some humorous Sherpa crept up and lifted the sack off the ground with his little finger. A few pieces of ironmongery equipment were later found inside it.

That evening Pierre Mazeaud and Michel Vaucher talked with Norman Dyhrenfurth and the first note of dissension over the running of the expedition arose. They complained that too few Sherpas were available to carry all the loads necessary for the West Ridge. Certainly more Face Sherpas than Ridge Sherpas were at Advance Base, the reason being that most of the Ridge men were assigned to carry the bulk of Ridge supplies from Base Camp through the Icefall to Camp I. Wolfgang Axt's plan was to make sure that a good store of essential loads was built up past the worst obstacle — the Icefall. It was not unreasonable to presume that under normal circumstances the carry through the Cwm would be simple. At this stage the two teams were functioning as separate expeditions, the equipment and manpower having been divided and allocated equally in the early days at Base Camp.

The Face Sherpas were more widely deployed between Base Camp and Camp II and John Evans was in the middle, able to coordinate the carries and to redirect his Sherpas where they were most needed at any particular moment. Wolfgang Axt had been out in front leading the climbing for most of the week and so the direction of the Ridge Sherpas had become somewhat haphazard. Norman Dyhrenfurth was not surprisingly unsympathetic to the plea for more Sherpas.

"The Americans all carried heavy loads in '63 because they're used to backpacking," explained Norman. "You'll just have to carry more yourselves if you haven't got the equipment up here. It's not like the Alps, you know."

To set an example and emphasize his point Norman started off alone next morning (April 18) in fine weather to descend to Camp I. He returned in the afternoon carrying two bottles of oxygen. As he was passing the Nuptse wall where the route lies close under the face in an area of fallen ice blocks, a powder avalanche came down very close to him.

CHAPTER 11

On April 18 Wolfgang Axt and Harsh Bahuguna had moved their camp a thousand feet (three hundred metres) higher to a sheltered site more suited for reaching Camp IV and the Japanese pair had gone up onto the Face accompanied by John Evans, who was carrying a load for them.

During the late afternoon, as he was coming slowly up the Cwm, Norman heard cries from high up towards the Western Shoulder. He shouted back and hurried on towards Advance Base Camp, suspecting something was wrong. The weather was closing in and visibility had become very poor so a strong Sherpa, Ang Lhakpa, started down from Camp II to look for Norman and help him in. Norman was very tired when he arrived.

Confined to my tent, I wrote long letters to Sarah describing sufficient of what I was doing to interest her yet not boldly enough to frighten her, sitting stoically at home with the children.

I had spent most of the afternoon chatting with Don Whillans in his tent. After a game of chess with Duane Blume, Don came to my tent to listen to some music. About 4:30 p.m. we reckoned a cup of tea would be welcome so we went outside; there we saw Wolfgang Axt.

He came into camp looking tired, ice was clinging to his eyebrows and beard, his parched lips were cracked and his woolly cap was covered in recently fallen snow.

Antony Thomas was the first person to meet him.

"Where's Harsh?"

"Oh, he's slow," Wolfgang replied. "He's not doing so well."

"Does he need help?" asked Antony.

"Perhaps."

From high up, far away to the left and out of vision because of the snow, a scream was heard.

"Go to Michel's tent and tell him Harsh needs to be rescued!" Antony spread the serious news quickly round the camp. Wolfgang seemed dazed but nevertheless sure that Harsh was following him.

Odd Eliassen quickly gathered his equipment and set off up the snow slope using ski sticks. He was closely followed by Michel Vaucher. Don Whillans had collected his climbing harness and all the ski sticks he could lay hands on and set off after Michel. John Evans returned after an exhausting day on the Face and rightly did not follow the rescue party but stayed back to prepare things for their return.

I collected my resuscitation kit and my medical High Box from my tent (they were fortunately in the only two medical trunks that had been sent up from Camp I). I called to the kitchen tent for one Sherpa to come with me as I did not know the route. Ang Purba came forward and took one High Box while I took the other one. I put on my crampons. I was wearing my heavy over-trousers and took my heavy, thick, red duvet jacket.

The time was 5:15 p.m. and the weather was worsening with heavy wind and drifting snow. Carlo Mauri, Pierre Mazeaud and I set off about the same time, following Don, who strode ahead placing the ski sticks at intervals in the snow as markers for our return. Michel and Odd were now over the moraine and going strongly up the ramp that lead towards the ice face under the West Ridge. I went well at first but we were going faster than normal and the effort at this height was terrible and breathing in the icy wind very difficult. We climbed up a small broken wall and onto a long, sloping sheet of ice and snow that was not very steep, but in the middle I got very afraid, being unroped, and just stopped for a few minutes, trying to get my breath and gather courage to push on up in the gathering darkness to Pierre, who was adjusting his crampon above me. I had a sight of Don about four hundred yards (three hundred and thirty metres) ahead, climbing the fixed rope at the end of the ice field. I caught up with Pierre but I was feeling very, very tired. The spindrift was blowing into everything but my hands were warm in my sealskin mittens. The ice field flattened out for 100 yards (91 metres) to the foot of the gash in the seracs where fixed ropes were placed for about 60 feet (18 metres). Climbing up was not too hard, but at the top there were twenty feet (six metres) of ice to crampon up. I did not like it without a rope.

Darkness had nearly fallen and a terrible wind was blowing down the mountain; I just leant against it and could barely hold myself upright with the ski poles. Pierre told me to put on another pullover and rest a moment. I took off my mittens and my anorak to put on the pullover and in the course of two minutes I lost all sensation in my fingers, which went dead and white. My feet were frozen. It was dark but we could still see the fixed rope behind us and just discern ahead a snow ramp along which we guessed the others must have gone, but we could not see or hear them in the howling wind.

Ang Purba went a few yards up to the crest of the slope to see if he could see anyone. He came back to say that there were three figures, one above, one in the middle and one below, about 100 yards (91 metres) away. We moved up and could see them too. I had a feeling I cannot explain, that if we went on we would never return; we were then at about 23,000 feet (7,000 metres) in a blizzard. I said goodbye to my wife and the children as I was sure we would die ... Unless I could warm my hands I could never help Harsh even if they could get him down, and the place we were in was steeply sloping and quite unsuitable for resuscitation. Pierre and I talked and agreed that the only thing possible to do was to descend the fixed ropes and build a platform where it was protected from the wind by some overhanging seracs. We would wait for fifteen to twenty minutes and if the others had not returned we would go back down. It was a horrible decision but the only one open to us. At least on a platform in the shelter of the wall I could do something by way of assistance to Harsh.

The descent of the fixed ropes in the dark terrified me, but Pierre helped me across the last few yards where the rope had finished. Two minutes later we heard Carlo descending, closely followed by Michel, Odd and Don. I just heard someone say, "Il est mort," and we met together at the foot of the slope and I cried and Odd cried too. Harsh had been a good friend and everyone liked him.

But the situation was still desperate for us, to find our way off the mountain in the bitter cold and pitch blackness. I went in the middle; we had three flashlights and we descended as fast as we could, all very tired. Twice I tripped and kicked my crampon off and had to adjust it with icy fingers, but everyone stopped to shine the torches so I could see. Lights came across the moraine and John Evans met us with a group of Sherpas and he broke down when he heard the news; he was an especially close friend of Harsh. About 10 p.m. we stumbled into the big kitchen bell tent physically and emotionally exhausted and many of us just cried our eyes out. The Sherpas made tea and soup, and gradually we recovered with the help of the medical whisky.

Then I learnt the story of what had gone on when they reached Harsh. Odd must have arrived first, perhaps twenty minutes before Pierre and I saw them from the top of the fixed rope. He said, "We've come to help you, Harsh. Are you okay?" and Harsh replied, "Yes," but Odd said he looked terrible. He was at the beginning of a section of fixed rope that protected a steep corner. He had come to an ice piton where he should have unclipped and clipped on again for the next section, which was apparently not very hard and less steep. But he had lost a glove and his rucksack was nearly off his shoulders and his clothes had been pulled up, exposing his belly. He was just hanging from the fixed rope, his hands frozen to it and his face coated in ice. Michel joined Odd. Together they tried to move Harsh sideways but it was impossible on the steep ice. So they began to lower him on the rope Odd had brought up, hoping he would reach a crevasse that lay about a hundred feet (thirty metres) below, where they could shelter him. Don arrived, having gone very fast, and he front-pointed with his crampons across to Harsh on bare ice without an axe or any rope protection. Harsh was at the end of the rope and had turned upside down. Don righted him but he said Harsh was blue in the face, unrecognizable, and his eyes were wide open, though he was still just groaning.

Don sized up the situation. The rope was too short to lower Harsh into the crevasse. He could only last another half-hour at most and was so far gone he could never survive the descent in the storm. Even if they had got him into the crevasse it is doubtful that anyone staying with him would have lasted the night, and to carry him down in the dark would have finished Harsh off as it would have taken at least seven to eight hours. Anyway, it was not possible, as all our fingers were freezing.

So Don took the only decision he could and a terrible one at that in the face of a companion who was still alive — even if only just. "Sorry Harsh, you've 'ad it," he said to himself and he left him and cramponned up to join the others. It must have been just before this that we sighted them, for not more than five minutes later we were all together at the bottom of the fixed rope and starting down.

I talked for a long time with Don later and he said that he had had a sudden feeling of certain knowledge that disaster was in the air for all six of us if we did not get quickly off the mountain. The others all felt it too. Certainly everyone had tried their hardest to save poor Harsh, but it was hopeless from the start as we set off too late and the weather was so bad.

The scene in the big bell tent was pitiable; crowded, hunched figures of Sherpas and members of the climbing party in the light of the hurricane lamp, all numbed and speechless; occasionally people giving their account of the disaster. We drifted off to bed after midnight. Odd asked if he could join me in my tent; I was delighted as I did not want to sleep alone. He is a fine man and was terribly upset, so we talked and wept long into the night and talked again when we awoke in the night and he was a wonderful companion. We talked of Harsh's family, fearing what it would be like for his poor wife, who did not yet know of the tragedy. Harsh had spoken so often of his girls and had just sent a cable for the birthday of one of them. How would they feel? Would they think it worthwhile that he died on Everest?

ODD AND I AGREED that the mountain was no more for us. Any secret ambition we might have had vanished with the death of Harsh. Fortunately I had a job to do and could stick to that and leave the others to climb the mountain. But for Odd the mountain was the sole reason he had come. We talked of our families and agreed that life was too precious to be abandoned for the sake of climbing to the top of this bloody mountain. And for what, anyway?

CHAPTER 12

After the death of Harsh Bahuguna the storm continued unabated for ten days. We were confined to the camp and spent most of the time in our tents trying to make the time pass quickly. Harsh was much in our minds, but we tried not to let the tragedy depress our spirits.

I wrote to Sarah at the time:

What does one do in a blizzard? Odd is in my tent still, thank goodness. We have been sleeping well, which is surprising as most people have a lot of trouble with sleep at this height. We wake about 6:30 a.m. and doze. The inside of the tent is covered with a thick rime of frost formed by the condensation of our breath; it gradually melts and drips on our sleeping bags which are fortunately quite impermeable. We talk about what is going to happen on the mountain, what we will do when we get home and how many more days away that is likely to be. Inside the lid of a flat cardboard inflatable splint box I have written out a calendar so I can tick the days off as they go by just as I used to, waiting for the end of term at boarding school. This is another way of diverting attention from our present unhappiness. Sona, one of the Sherpa cooks, brings a cup of tea at 7:30 with a cheerful, "Good morning, morning tea." He has been up for two hours already melting the snow for the water. How he manages out there in the cold wind I can't imagine but he is always cheerful, always polite. Camomile tea is all we have but Mrs. Rabbit found a dose was good for Peter when he had a cold, though we were not lucky like Flopsy, Mopsy and Cottontail who had "bread and milk and blackberries for their supper."

I have to pass water so I use my plastic urine bottle inside my sleeping bag; all last night's contribution has frozen and sedimented, looking as if I have some terrible kidney disease. We hear the banging of the breakfast gong and get up — not moving too fast or we get breathless. I have borrowed Odd's reindeer skin boots for the night and they shed moulting hairs all round the tent. I pull on my own leather inner boots that I have kept under my pillow to prevent them getting frozen. Then a very clumsy and heavy pair of outers have to be laced up.

We unzip the door flap and outside snow has piled up against the tent and is drifting two feet deep. The big white army bell tent is only 20 yards away from us. We dash across to get out of the wind and snow as quickly as possible for it is bitterly cold. I double up and crawl through the wind-tunnel entrance. Several people are already inside so I say, "Good morning" — what irony! — and I try to find a rope to sit on, or a tin or a corner of a Sherpa's mattress if I am very lucky. The paraffin stoves which stand on some flint rocks in the centre of the tent round the pole are burning hard trying to melt lumps of snow in large aluminium pans. We sit hunched and clutching our knees, the tent warms up and drips fall down our necks. The canvas floor is wet and pools form in depressions and bits of rubbish gather with the dregs of tea that have been emptied out on the floor. My feet become colder and colder and I try to wriggle my toes but it doesn't do much good and I can barely feel them, just a vaguely wooden feeling as though they belong to someone else.

The tent fills slowly. Carlo Mauri's leonine face appears in the entrance, his beard and face whitened by a sprinkling of snow and his moustache bristling with ice crystals.

"Buon giorno," he beams a warm smile.

"Où est Pierre?" we ask.

"Il dort encore," replies Carlo. Pierre Mazeaud is a great sleeper. He can lie in his tent for hours on end passing the time in a vacuum. This is a great quality for a climber on mountains such as these where many days have to be passed in tents sitting out bad weather.

Wide-visored goggles pushed up onto a wool balaclava thrust through the tunnel entrance followed by a small figure in an all-in-one sky-blue nylon down suit with a small union jack over the left breast. He could be a driver from a grand prix circuit crawling out of the pits.

"Mornin' all," he grunts without removing the cigar from the corner of his mouth even during a bout of coughing. Don Whillans has been through all this sort of thing before so often that there is little new under the sun for him and our present discomforts are all an accepted part of his life as a professional mountaineer.

Yvette Vaucher comes in followed by Michel. Even at 22,000 feet [6,700 metres] she maintains her charm and attractiveness. The theoretical problems posed by having one woman in an all-male party are exploded by Yvette. Her own personality apart, the fact that she is a woman helps to maintain the tone of conversation and manners on a higher level than when rough tough men are living together under close contact and trying circumstances; then mundane politeness takes on added importance. Nothing is more conducive to irritation than incivility, be it bad language or uncontrolled passing of wind. Some members were peculiarly prone to lapses in etiquette and coughing, hawking, spitting and farting happened regardless of place or persons. In the company of Yvette, though far from prudish herself, standards tended to be maintained and we were grateful for this. Michel is strong, experienced and well-balanced with a smile as soft as his wife's.

A sleepy little figure dressed like a jockey just dismounted at Tokyo racecourse giggles his greeting. Naomi Uemura is five feet tall, wears his red wool hat with the black peak turned up over one ear and a voluminous pair of baggy yellow windproof trousers. His conversation runs in jerky spasms of pidgin English or occasionally French, punctuated at intervals with a burst of mirth.

He is as inscrutable as his young friend Reizo Ito who speaks few words of any-one's language but looks so like the Sherpas that he forms a bond with them. Both Japanese will sleep for twenty hours at a stretch when there is nothing better to do, so we are surprised to see them up on this inclement morning.

Norman Dyhrenfurth appears, well groomed, every hair in place even here — a bronzed Apollo belying his years.

"It was never like this with AMEE [the American Mount Everest Expedition of 1963, of which Norman was the leader]; bad days could be counted on the fingers of one hand then."

The Sherpas remember clearly the few occasions they saw clouds with the Indians in 1965 and with successive days of fine weather they got nine men on top. Naomi, twice here with the Japanese, recalls a few bad days but no continuous storms.

Norman continues, "I've never seen such weather. There is more ice on the mountain and fewer fine days at Base Camp than I ever remember."

So we sit round like an English tea party and discuss the weather as there is little else we want to talk about, and beyond the buffeted walls of the tent the whiteout continues.

The discussion draws to a close as Ang Pema and Sona hand round porridge, and we add nuts and raisins and then camomile tea again.

After breakfast a dreaded moment arrives. The wind outside is swirling the snow round the camp and I can just see the lower part of the Face through breaks in the cloud and snow. The latrine area is behind a little hillock a few yards only from camp and already quite foul, as there is no suitable crevasse that can be straddled. But for a few days it is gratefully covered by new snowfall — the only reason we have to be thankful for it. First I undo my thick outer trousers, having difficulty with the metal zip that is frozen and sticks to my fingers, which are so cold they make clumsy work of fumbling with the catch. Then I drop my purple jeans and long underpants and squat. My backside becomes insensible and a fine layer of spindrift fills my pants. What a joy to pull them up as soon as the deed is done and try to restore sen-sation to frozen cheeks. Even this performance takes the breath out of me and I walk slowly back to camp using a ski stick to probe the ground ahead to avoid falling into the hidden crevasse beside which the path goes.

Some people are standing about listening to Duane Blume's radio schedule with Base; peeps and crackles and the occasional burst of voice break through but reception is very poor in the storm. There is no point in hanging around in this weather, so I take my hot water bottle to Ang Pema who will fill it with water when he has any on the boil and bring it over to my tent. I tidy up a little, put my feet into my sleeping bag, prop myself up against the medicine box, try to warm my hands and get my pen working so that I can start writing. Odd comes in and makes himself comfortable on the other side of the tent. There is not much room for manoeuvring so one person lies still while the other one moves about. I draw a picture of Bleinau Uchaf, our farmhouse in South Wales, and we talk about it, about fishing and camping in Norway and about journeys we have made in the Sahara, he in the Hoggar, I in Tibesti. Then with the small map in his pocket diary we plan journeys for the future. Then we start writing home to the sound of the tape recorder playing "Sentimental Susan."

Soon it will be lunch — cold feet again — then the bag. Read a little poetry, the Odyssey (wish I had something lighter), then supper. Much of the time I just lie on my bag staring at the ridge pole of the tent. How it doesn't bend in this wind I can't think. We have a chat in the bell tent after supper. Then bed at 7 p.m. and Odd and I have a long talk about Harsh again. Then we sleep and twelve hours later start another day.

The storm eventually blew itself out but those miserable days were passed in trying to sleep through the whine of the wind and the flapping of tents. I moved from tent to tent talking with friends to help the time speed by. I played chess with Duane Blume and found a kindred spirit who was as homesick as I was and delighted to talk about his family and have a gentle moan about the hell we had let ourselves in for.

Odd Eliassen and I talked a lot about Harsh and looked for some justification in his pointless death. Wolfgang Axt stayed alone in his tent and I visited him and encouraged him to talk. He knew that people thought he bore some responsibility for the accident, and he did not feel this was justified. He came and wept in my tent and we played chess to take our minds off the terrible burden that hung on us all, especially on Wolfgang. But no one censured him; no one cut him off however violent his feelings and I think we all felt deep sympathy for him in his suffering at losing his best friend, a sad memory he would bear for the rest of his life. We were made acutely aware how appropriate was the cliché "there but for the grace of God go I," both in regard to Wolfgang's grief and Harsh's death.

Naomi Uemura and Reizo Ito had come down from Camp III on April 20 because of the bad weather and Naomi was very upset by the news of the death of Harsh, who had been his close friend. That day and the next Gary Colliver left Camp II with a relief party, trying to link up with Camp I in order to bring food and fuel, but they were turned back halfway down the Cwm by the appalling weather. Duane Blume tried to keep his regular schedules on the radio, which he was now supervising with enthusiasm and efficiency, but all he could receive were crackles and distorted voices and no coherent contact was made. We were cut off and had to make the best of it.

We had a sing-song after our meagre dinner in the bell tent and spirits began to rise. Men laughed for the first time in days and shed the gloom and oppression that had burdened us all. Michel Vaucher conducted a roundelay in which people took the parts of various instruments of the orchestra, making characteristic noises and gestures in the chorus. The Sherpas howled with laughter, although bassoons and violas were far beyond the reach of their experience.

I did a "Yeti hunt," translating it into Nepali. All the words and gestures of the leader are followed in his quest until the Yeti is found and then the action is reversed at speed as one runs away to escape its clutches. I collapsed breathless from exertion and laughing at the end and we turned to singing national songs. That sing-song really bound us together in our adversity.

"When will this weather clear?" I asked Kanchha, who was on Everest in 1953, as we sat sharing a coil of rope and drinking unsweetened camomile tea, the sugar having run out.

"This is the Sherpa monsoon," he replied. "Many times we have bad storms before the real monsoon. They say the potatoes are being planted down in Namche now, so maybe we won't have clear weather again before the monsoon comes in the middle of May."

We talked of his visits to Lhasa, where his father carried on business before the Chinese came.

"What was the Potala like?" I asked, envious of a man who had seen such a wonder of the world.

"Big, on a high hill," Kanchha replied, "and many trees and gardens down below."

I described the dzongs of Bhutan that I imagined were similar to those in Tibet and told him of my journey there with my family.

"Better holiday than this one, doctor sa'b," he observed, and I heartily agreed with him.

"How much longer can this storm go on?" I asked.

"*Kuni?*" he replied with a shrug of his shoulders and an upward twist of his hand. "Who knows?" — or cares.

Monsoon weather is usually remarkably predictable.

As summer advances the land mass of Central Asia heats up, the warm air rises and leaves an area of low atmospheric pressure into which is drawn cooler, vapour-laden oceanic air from the Bay of Bengal. Between the hot plains of India and the upland plateau of Tibet lie the Himalayas. As the moist, northward-moving air meets this barrier it is pushed upwards and condenses to form cloud; when the clouds meet the cold upper atmosphere, precipitation occurs and rain falls on the southern slopes of the mountains.

Before the monsoon breaks the pattern of weather is of high banks of cumulus building up in the afternoon over the mountains, followed by short thunderstorms. But in the monsoon, which lasts usually from June to September, the mountains are perpetually covered in cloud and rain is heavy and steady.

Perhaps I was trying to fool myself — at that moment all I wanted to do was to get the hell out of this awful spot and go back home to my family. Feeling very homesick, I wrote to Sarah:

> I guess we will be leaving here on May 21st, not a day later. But Norman keeps reckoning on June 1st. That could be possible, but very lucky. Much better to err on the early side and be pleasantly surprised if you get a few extra days' grace. In 1936 on the north side the monsoon came three weeks early and the expedition was a wash out. If you remember in Bhutan we had a snow storm in Bumthang on Adam's birthday, March 21st; then good weather, but the monsoon had really set in when we crossed the Rudong La about the middle of April. I can see us now trying to dry the children out in that cave at Menjibi when we were all soaked to the skin. And that became a regular daily performance till we reached the East in early May. But the monsoon weather from Bhutan takes a couple of weeks to move up, so it would arrive here a little later. Apparently this winter has been abnormally mild all over the world so we can expect an abnormal season here.

Following the inquiry the day after Harsh Bahuguna's death, we had all stated our preferences concerning what should happen in the future; Mazeaud and Mauri mentioned the South Col, the Vauchers and Axt were for sticking to the Ridge, Odd Eliassen and I felt all effort should be concentrated on the Face.

The Face team were busy planning for the break in the weather that everyone felt must come. John Evans held long discussions with Don Whillans, Naomi Uemura and John Cleare, the BBC cameraman, making calculations on scraps of paper of what would be needed in order to push a team to the foot of the rock wall high on the Face from where the difficult break for the summit would have to be made. They gave an impression that when their moment came they would be ready to throw themselves back into the attack.

Among the Ridge team no such unanimity existed. The idea of a switch to the South Col route had grown in intensity and a meeting was held with Norman Dyhrenfurth to discuss the case. We met in sunshine on the first clear day after the storm, outside Norman's tent beside the miserable little pile of West Ridge equipment. Away on the snow slopes leading to the Western Shoulder we could see a black dot, the body of our friend Harsh Bahuguna hanging on the end of a rope. We all felt the gap that he should have filled in our team. His was always a quiet, considered voice in our discussions, expressing sound and experienced opinion. Because of the recent heavy snow we could not yet bring him down.

The Vauchers had joined Mazeaud and Mauri in their preference for a change to the South Col for several reasons. The West Ridge was in very bad condition due to the heavy plastering of snow on the mountain, which made it too dangerous. Time was running out and an early monsoon was forecast, therefore we had a better chance of climbing the mountain by the South Col in ten days and maybe putting the whole team on top; the West Ridge would take much longer and probably only one pair would reach the summit. Those Sherpas of the Ridge team who were at Advance Base said they preferred to go to the South Col; the ground was easier and Kanchha, the sirdar, had already been six times to the South Col and knew the ground well. It was pointed out that the West Ridge had already been climbed by the Americans in 1963 and Norman's insistence on the "true" West Ridge being a new route was splitting hairs. Finally, one of the aims of the expedition was to put a woman on top of Everest, and by going to the South Col this might be achieved.

Wolfgang Axt was still in favour of the West Ridge although he felt very depressed after the accident. Michel Vaucher had replaced him as coordinator and it is greatly to Wolfgang's credit that he showed no bitterness at this inevitable decision by Norman Dyhrenfurth. Wolfgang pointed out that much of the groundwork had been laid for the West Ridge and we should continue on it for the sake of Harsh.

Odd and I had already expressed our view, immediately after the inquiry, that the Ridge should be abandoned and all efforts directed towards the Face, thinking that it was preferable to fail honourably on the principal route we had come to climb than to succeed where twenty-three men in five successful expeditions had trodden their way to the top of Everest.

Norman asked for a vote. It ended up four to one for the South Col with two abstentions; Odd Eliassen was definitely against going to the South Col but wanted time to discuss the matter with Jon Teigland (still at Base along with David Isles and Juréc Surdel), while I made it clear I had definitely lost interest in the climbing and intended to stick to the job I had come to do.

Norman Dyhrenfurth was prepared to accept a majority decision. When it came, he said that he would give all his support and help, and plans for an assault on the South Col were begun immediately. Sitting there we could see every feature of the South Col route, the Lhotse face, the Geneva Spur, the Col itself and the South Ridge, which was partly hidden till it joined the South Summit, and then there was the top. Such a temptingly short way off but a world away and the frustration of many good men before us. I found this "easy way to the top in ten days" hard to comprehend, looking at the three oxygen bottles, empty food cases and a few coils of rope that lay in our team's pile.

That evening radio contact was made with the other camps. David Isles, who was stuck at Camp I, said he was still for the Ridge, Camp III was already up, Camp IV was nearly established and he saw no reason to retreat and good reasons for going on for Harsh's sake. At Base Jon Teigland, having been given only one minute to make up his mind, said he was pre-pared to go with the majority and Juréc Surdel wanted to stay on the Ridge. So the vote fell to go to the South Col and that decision was final.

April 24 dawned bright again and a large party set off across the gla-cier to attempt to recover Harsh Bahuguna's body.

They found the body still hanging from the ropes as it had been left but now covered in snow and frozen over. The members of the original rescue team who were in the recovery party had to steel themselves to cover the same ground and to relive the awful experience of that black night. The day remained clear and, with a large number of climbers and Sherpas to help, the grisly task was accomplished in seven hours under perfect conditions. A week before if we had attempted such a recovery with Harsh alive in a blizzard by night with only a handful of men, the possibility of success would without doubt have been nil and the dangers to those involved frightening to contemplate.

At the same time I set off with John Evans, Reizo Ito and two Sherpas to break trail towards Camp III. Snow of the past week still covered the tents that just pushed their orange heads out of a white blanket. Even after a day of sun consolidating the fall we sank thigh deep into the snow. One man would push ahead for 100 yards (91 metres) and would then bend exhausted and panting over his ice axe while another took over the lead.

Snowshoes would have saved all this labour and I thought of my own pair, made by a Naskaupi Indian, that lay in the basement at home with dust on them. Light aluminium racquets with nylon strings about half the normal size would be ideal, as this problem recurs with every snowfall. The use of skis was debated before we left Europe and I think the decision not to bring them was correct. Although the touring style of ski would be good in the Western Cwm, especially if used with attachable skins for climbing, skis are cumbersome and awkward to carry all the way from Kathmandu for such a brief spell of use. One American did ski right down the Icefall in 1963 and in 1970 one member of the Japanese ski team descended from the South Col at speeds approaching 90 miles (144 kilometres) an hour, using a parachute for braking.

After an hour we were still only a quarter of a mile from camp and away on the other side of the Everest basin we could see a line of figures toiling their way upwards. When the clouds opened the sun came out and beat down on the snow, which threw back intense rays that burnt the undersides of our nostrils and cheeks. We approached a crevassed area deeply covered with new snowfall that left only small depressions in the even contour to indicate the chasms hidden beneath, whereas before they had been quite easily visible.

"Shouldn't we use a rope here, John?" I suggested. "I'm a bit chicken crossing ground like this when we can't really see what's underneath."

"Sure thing, Pete," John Evans replied. "I guess we'd better send one of the Sherpas back for one."

So we sat down on our rucksacks and waited for half an hour while young Kanchha Kunde went off to fetch the rope. The track having been made already, he soon returned and we started into the crevassed area all tied on. As we drew nearer to the bergschrund, the big crevasse that runs across the foot of the Face where the glacier is detached from the mountain, the faces of Everest and of Lhotse loomed over us and seemed very steep and overbearing. I enjoyed the climb, it being the first proper exercise I had taken since the onset of the storm, and although the effort needed was heavy, I was happy to be out of the oppressive confinement of the camp and the horrible sickly orange light of my tent. John and Reizo were pleasant companions and my morale rose from the depths into which it had fallen in the previous days.

On reaching the bergschrund we sat and ate some raisins. The time was three o'clock and we decided not to attempt to reach Camp III as we were not equipped to spend the night there. So we ran back in our hard-made tracks and reached Camp II as the others were returning, dragging the body of Harsh attached by climbing ropes. They laid him down 100 yards (91 metres) below camp and erected a canvas cover over him. The sun went down at the end of the Cwm and as it dropped behind the shoulder of Nuptse shafts of light like bright spokes shone for a few seconds and then died away, leaving a deep red sky; in the same way the life of our friend Harsh Bahuguna had been extinguished a few days before. Looking at the still heap lying a little way off it was impossible to believe that this was all that remained of our friendly, enthusiastic companion whose soft voice we would hear no more.

Once more gloom came down on the camp and laughter seemed quite inappropriate so long as he was there. Odd and I talked again of Harsh's wife, who by now would know the awful news, and we thought of his two little girls — their unmeasurable grief and the incomprehensible truth

John Evans in the Icefall (JOHN CLEARE)

Face of Nuptse (JOHN CLEARE)

Crevasse bridge (JOHN CLEARE)

Carlo Mauri in the Icefall

Icefall ladders

Camp II

Harsh Bahuguna with Sherpas (JOHN CLEARE)

Bringing Harsh Bahuguna's body down (JOHN CLEARE)

Exit (JOHN CLEARE)

that Daddy would never return to throw them in the air and catch them again, to read them stories or kiss them goodnight. We knew that it could easily have been one of us lying there frozen in the snow and inwardly we thanked God, knowing that we were not yet out of danger and that it could yet happen to us or to another friend of ours. What a waste! He had barely started on the mountain that he had come to climb.

ON THE 25TH the weather was bad again and another party set off from Camp II to try to link up with those men bringing food up from Camp I. Again no liaison was made with Camp I where David Peterson and David Isles were cut off and holding out on their own with a large cache of supplies that had been brought through the Icefall but could be moved no farther.

Food was becoming scarce and we were reduced to eating porridge without sugar for breakfast, biscuits and chocolate for lunch and dehydrated soup for supper with a little foul tinned meat until that ran out. This was no diet for men to perform a hard day's work on, and I am sure contributed to everyone's lethargy and the onset of the outbreak of sickness that was soon to fall on the camp.

The storm raged outside and morale sank lower and lower as we sat round in the bell tent, looking for a corner of a Sherpa mattress or an empty tin to squat on and trying to avoid the drips of condensation from the roof.

The wind in the night was violent but my tent was well pinned down by snow that had drifted to a depth of two feet (sixty centimetres) round the outer fly sheet. It pressed so hard that the floor space inside was narrowed and Odd and I were pushed closer and closer towards the centre. With this weight of snow the tent was in danger of collapsing so we got hold of two shovels and began to dig it out. We both felt dizzy and breathless with even a little exertion as we had been lying about doing nothing for several days, but the Sherpas around us seemed to manage with little effort, and during this arduous time at Camp II they never lost their sense of humour and cheerfulness.

Our food supplies were fast being eaten and fuel for cooking had almost gone so Michel Vaucher and Gary Colliver set off with a party of Sherpas to try to reach Camp I in the hope of collecting loads from men coming up from there. The scene resembled one of Edward Wilson's watercolours painted on Scott's expedition; a long line of goggled men with ski poles, bent over and leaning into the wind, could be seen disappearing into the thickly falling snow. Their progress was laborious and slow, the leading man having to wade thigh deep in powdered snow to make new tracks, the old ones having been covered over. That day they returned after five hours of fruitless work, having failed to reach Camp I because of the depth of the snow that covered the crevasses from view and the danger of avalanches from the Lhotse face.

I wrote to Sarah:

I can honestly say I have rarely enjoyed two weeks less in my life than those at Camp II. Maybe one day in a warm oblivious afterglow, when painful memories are forgotten and I can only remember the glorious moments, they will mellow and be put down to experience. But if the truth be reported, the storm, fatigue and hunger coming after the Harsh tragedy all added up to one thing — sheer misery.

CHAPTER 13

On April 25 Michel Vaucher complained that he had felt a pain in his calf for two days, so I examined him as carefully as one can when sprawled inside a Whillans box with snow blowing in through the zip. He felt acute tenderness down the middle four inches (ten centimetres) of his calf over the popliteal vein. I felt sure that he had an early phlebitis, an inflammation of the vein wall, which is a recognized complication of altitude.

Michel was not the sort of person to make a fuss, but he felt confident that the pain was deep in the leg and not just the ache of an overstrained muscle that he might well have had after his efforts of the past few days. He said that he had noticed it the previous day when they had gone to bring Harsh Bahuguna down. When he was climbing on the front points of his crampons, kicking them into the ice to get a hold, he felt a deep ache in his right calf.

He offered me some nuts and I brought my tape recorder to his tent so he could listen to some music while he was resting with his leg raised on a pillow. I went off to Duane Blume's tent to play chess and discuss the problem with him in order to get some much-needed reassurance. Phlebitis can occur through lying around in tents, taking no exercise, and we had all had plenty of that during recent days. With the muscles being inactive, blood is not pumped along the veins as efficiently as normally and becomes static. Duane checked his records of blood tests that he had carefully measured for physiological studies since we left Kathmandu and he found that Michel's hematocrit, the measure of the number of cells in the blood, had increased by 36 percent whereas the average increase for the expedition was 23 percent. This fact added weight to the diagnosis, which was serious, more for its possible complications than for the painful leg itself. When the vein is inflamed the viscous blood is more likely to stick to the wall and form a clot, or thrombus. If this happens pieces can break off and emboli can lodge in small terminal vessels of the lung.

I did not want to alarm Michel and I knew he was the last person who would readily leave the mountain, but I felt sure he should go down to Base Camp for a while. I returned in the afternoon and examined his leg again, confirming my diagnosis. The leg was not swollen, the diameters of his calves were equal and his temperature was normal, so I felt sure the vein was in the very early stages of inflammation and that early treatment would prevent the danger of complications.

"I know you don't want to go down, Michel, but I think it would be safer to be at Base Camp for a week to try to get this thing to settle," I explained. "If it does then I see no reason why you shouldn't come back up again. What do you think Yvette will say?" Yvette was away setting up Camp III under the Lhotse face with Carlo Mauri, Pierre Mazeaud and some Sherpas.

Michel, a mathematics teacher in a high school in Geneva, is as gentle as he is strong and his French speech as soft as his manners. His record of difficult and original Alpine ascents is formidable and has won him a certificate as a professional mountain guide, an honour much cherished in Switzerland. He was a member of the Swiss expedition to Dhaulagiri I in 1960 and had distinguished himself as a climber who could acclimatize well at altitude.

He and Yvette were a fine advertisement for marriage; she is five years older than Michel and was a widow when they were married in 1963. Together they have done many hard climbs and have been through some desperate situations.

"I love Michel and I love mountains and that is why I am here," she once said with a warm smile.

The poignancy of this statement was well understood by those of us who saw tears of joy welling from her eyes as she caught her first view of the Himalayas through the porthole window of the airplane approaching Kathmandu.

Yvette has also trained as a parachutist, but she belies the toughness that hides behind the strong bone structure of her attractive face. We all loved Yvette. Since the day in Kathmandu when she was put in charge of the expedition postcards she only had to smile at the men once to make them get down to signing a pile of several hundred cards.

Much of Yvette's leisure time with Michel has been spent in the company of men in the rough environment of climbing huts. But this has in no way hardened her and she maintained her femininity under circumstances when many a woman would not try, adding a beneficial softening influence on this otherwise all-male party.

"She'll take your advice, as I will," he replied. "I've had this sort of trouble before and I don't want to take any risks. She'll probably come down with me." Michel had spent a night out in a bivouac with Yvette on the north face of the Dent Blanche and had got bad frostbite of his feet, for which he had a bilateral sympathectomy operation to increase the blood flow in his legs. Yvette had escaped physically unharmed from this ordeal.

"I think I should accompany you down to Base Camp to see nothing happens. Dave Peterson will be coming up here when he can get through so all the camps will be medically covered," I said.

I had also been trying to treat Gary Colliver, John Cleare, Pin Howell and Wolfgang Axt for bronchitis that was moving towards broncho-pneumonia. Crawling into small tents, battling through layers of clothing to get at the chest and listen with an icy stethoscope was an ineffectual way of treating sick men.

I explained the situation to Norman, who was himself lying in his tent suffering from laryngitis that had prevented him from speaking properly during his stay at Camp II. This had been made worse by shouting up to Harsh Bahuguna, on his return up the Cwm alone from Camp I carrying the two oxygen bottles, when he heard Harsh calling for help. I was keen not to appear to order anyone down. I preferred to let people take their own decisions after fully discussing their problem, in the hope of avoiding repercussions later. A very easy way out of a tricky situation is to say, "Oh, but my doctor sent me down," and "doctor's orders" has a strange mystique.

"I think I ought to escort the sick people down to Base when the weather clears as they aren't going to get better up here and all they can do is lie around in their tents eating up food that is scarce enough anyway," I said.

"That seems reasonable to me," Norman replied.

"In fact," I went on, "I think we might be wise to move all the serious medical work down to Base, where we have really good facilities compared with the lousy conditions here. The delay in evacuating anyone from here would be compensated by their improved chances of recovery off the Hill. How long do you think it would take by toboggan?" We had two sledge stretchers for the purpose of mountain rescue.

"I suppose with a team of Sherpas changing round you could get to Camp I in two or three hours. Then the upper part of the Icefall might be difficult but the second toboggan could come up from Base to Dump Camp. If the pressure was on, it could probably be done in six hours," he replied.

"Well, Dave Peterson will come on up here to look after the Face and he can send anyone sick down to Base."

"How sick is 'sick'?" said Norman.

"I think our criterion of sickness should be when a man can't manage a full day's work. If I treat them intensively down there I think we've a better chance of getting them back up the Hill," I said.

I spent a full hour discussing these problems with Norman. I liked talking with him as he is a warm and sympathetic man and has a deep feeling for people and the expedition for which he has worked so assiduously. The past days had been bad enough for us but they must have been far worse for Norman, seeing his dream vanishing before his very eyes.

During the night I felt feverish and started coughing and by morning was sick myself. A howling wind greeted us and several tents were in the throes of being blown down, but we decided to go on down to try to reach Camp I to get food and to take down the sick. The possibility of having to evacuate the whole party down to Camp I was becoming more and more of a reality and many people felt that if this happened it would be the end of the expedition. I dressed in all my heavy clothing, put on my thick down mittens and stuffed a few things in a duffle bag as there was the usual rush at the last moment to get away. Drifts had formed round the Camp and I could just see a file of Sherpa figures and the sick men disappearing into the blizzard. I collected Michel and Yvette and we set off. The hours that ensued were horrible.

A biting wind cut across our faces despite the wolverine-fur lining of our hoods and it was often so strong we just stopped in our tracks and leant into it against our ski sticks to avoid being blown over. The spindrift of fine, blown snow penetrated our necks, wrists and boots, adding to the cold. I later wrote to Sarah, "God, I was miserable and frightened, too, as I felt so weak." I coughed and coughed, partly from inhaling the fine snow and partly from the bug I must have caught by being coughed over in small tents by the invalids.

We took Harsh's body down with us, wrapped in one of the medical rescue bags. One Sherpa went ahead to break the trail through thick new snow and then followed six others with Harsh; accompanying our friend on his last journey increased our unhappiness. The fine snow was blowing so thickly across the ground that the tracks of the man in front were being filled up before his companion following could plant his feet in them. When I stopped for rests I just crouched down in a ball to avoid being bowled over, turned my face sideways and panted. I felt very weak and was sure I was sickening for something, so I thought it was a good thing I was going down. Yvette followed behind me and I was ashamed to be so feeble when she was forging along uncomplaining and with such strength — and our track was all downhill.

I thought to myself, "What will I do if we don't make contact with Camp I or if the way is blocked? I just don't have the strength to return to Camp II. Poor Scott, Oates, Wilson, Bowers. What hell they must have been through. Days and days of this. At least we know we are not far from our rescuers. They had none."

About 1 p.m. we met the party from Camp I on the avalanche patch at the foot of the Lhotse face. Our Sherpas had some sarcastic things to say about the fact that we had managed to get down three-quarters of the way; they exchanged loads and the poor fellows had to turn round and return to Camp II with Don Whillans and John Evans. I met Dave Peterson and explained what the new medical routine was to be. He told me he had found three packets of cigarettes that I was keeping in my box left at Camp I and had shared them with the Sherpas, as they had run out.

I did not like the bridges we had to cross before Camp I as the crevasses had widened. It was a huge relief to stumble into Camp I and find Murray Sayle there, his chin sprouting grey hairs, thinner, but cheerful as usual. Michel, Yvette, Pin and I decided to spend the night there and go down the Icefall next day after a night's rest. Wolfgang, Gary and John Cleare thought they would press on down to reach Base. I doubted the wisdom of this as they would be lucky to get down by nightfall and they were tired and not well.

I crawled into my sleeping bag in Murray's tent and did not move until next morning. Murray was wildly untidy but very punctilious about who occupied whose half of the tent. He had just been sharing it for a week with Harka Bahadur Gurung, a Nepali geographer, who had told him folklore horror stories to brighten up his evenings, while Murray had twice given him the history of the economic politics of Japan. Murray was now on volume 6 of Gibbon. The floor of the tent had a large hole beneath it where the crevasse had been gradually opening up and we manoeuvred for space to avoid sinking into this, but still maintaining strict neutrality over our frontier. We laughed a great deal during the evening, did a lot of talking and I filled in some details of what had been happening upstairs. A cheerful Sherpa face appeared at our tent with a bowl of hot soup and we quietly scoffed a tin of salmon that Sona Girme, our sirdar, produced.

The following morning we set off about 10:00 a.m. — Yvette, Michel, Pin and myself. Pin went very slowly, which was a relief as it gave me chances to rest; I was feeling very feeble and coughing up a lot of foul yellow phlegm. The Icefall was unrecognizable so great were the changes in it; snow bridges had disappeared, crevasses had opened up and seracs had toppled over. The devastated area below the topmost lip of the Cwm had caved in like a sponge cake that has sunk in the middle. The large crevasse had stretched beyond the length of the aluminium ladder that was now suspended by an added section of another ladder which did not fit securely and swayed. The handrail was no longer taut and leaned out-wards. I thought of the wire-rope man in the circus doing his tricks and I could have wished for his safety net.

A lone figure appeared below and we caught sight of and lost him as he wound in and out of seracs. As he approached we recognized the thrust-forward jaw and the mat of hair under which hid Dougal Haston, lone as usual and going fast after his rest at Base. We stopped to chat for ten minutes — or rather Michel and Yvette did, while Pin and I bent over our ice axes and coughed and hawked, trying to clear our lungs and get back our breath. Then Dougal forged on to rejoin Don. I was thankful to reach the flat ground at the bottom of the Icefall and to feel that I was out of danger from seracs, crevasses and all the other horrible things about that place.

When I reached Base Camp on April 27 I felt ready to join the ranks of the invalids already gathered there. John Cleare, Gary Colliver, Pin Howell and Wolfgang Axt had chest and throat troubles and I started intensive work on them. We held clinics twice a day in the hospital; each man spent five minutes inhaling steam from a pan with a large plastic bag over his head to retain the vapour. Ang Tsering kept a kettle boiling in one corner to replenish the brew. As soon as the steam breathing was over the patient moved across to my bed, vacating the seat at the desk for the next man, and lay on his front with a pillow under his middle and his head near the floor. Ang Tsering and I beat and pummelled his chest in a manner that was more akin to flogging than the refined modern physiotherapy at which we were aiming in our amateur way.

The atmosphere was convivial and the men felt better and returned for more. I gave antibiotics to those who had pus in their sputum and within a day or two I began to notice an improvement in the general condition of the patients with pneumonia.

Chest problems become much more serious at altitude. Any condition that lowers the efficiency of a lung that is only just managing to cope with the low oxygen pressure and the thinness of the air throws an unbearable strain on the breathing. For this reason, as soon as a man was over the acute stage of his illness, when his temperature had come down to normal, his sputum was clear of pus and the sounds in his chest were healthier, I encouraged him to go down the valley to Thyangboche or Kunde to recuperate. I was subsequently criticized in the newspapers by people knowing nothing of medicine, for allegedly being too soft in allowing climbers to go down sick and encouraging a state of mass hypochondria that contributed to the final unsuccess of the expedition. The naïveté of these pontifical statements was evident to anyone with even a slight comprehension of the problem; for me, having worked hard to get people fit to return to the scene of action, they were frankly abrasive. Of the twelve people evacuated to Base Camp in May, seven were returned to the Hill and were able to do some support work even if not yet in prime condition.

CHAPTER 14

Everything seemed to be against us and the expedition that had begun so auspiciously had now run up against big problems, most of them outside our control.

We were nearly a month late in our schedule owing to the bad state of the Icefall, which had taken so long to crack open, and to the blizzard that had marooned us at Advance Base Camp for nearly two weeks. The death of our friend Harsh Bahuguna was superimposed on the problems of time and weather, and the start of an incipient wave of illness combined to lower the morale and fitness of the team.

Another difficulty began to creep in for the first time — personal discontent. And like a cancer it grew from a small beginning and spread, affecting the whole body. To understand the full picture of what happened is extremely difficult. So many people have made public comment based on inadequate fact and so many inaccurate stories have been told by the press in the aftermath of the expedition.

The evening of April 27, when Michel and Yvette Vaucher, Pin Howell and I arrived at Base Camp, we learnt about conversations over the radio between Camp II and Base Camp the previous night.

Norman Dyhrenfurth had reconsidered the whole situation in the light of the number of men who had gone down sick, and asked for another vote. Pierre Mazeaud and Carlo Mauri were still for the South Col. The Norwegian pair and David Isles wanted to give their support to the Face team only. Wolfgang Axt wanted to return to Camp II when he was fit, to bring down Camp III West; he said he did not want to go on the Face because he had promised his wife that he would not do so. The Vauchers and I had been at Camp I, where no radio contact could be made. David Peterson told Norman Dyhrenfurth that Michel Vaucher would never come up the mountain again and so could be effectively discounted from the climb.

On the result of the vote, Norman said that he would put the decision about the South Col route to Jimmy Roberts to act as final arbiter and invited Pierre Mazeaud and Carlo Mauri to join the Face team.

"I am not going to be a Sherpa and carry for Anglo-Saxons," Pierre Mazeaud was reported as saying. "It is not only me but France you have insulted."

Pierre and Carlo vehemently expressed their discontent and came down to Base Camp next day (April 29) carrying some of their personal equipment. They talked with the Vauchers and together decided to leave the expedition. Norman asked them to put off a final decision until Jimmy Roberts' return.

All four were very angry about the vote of the previous day. The Vauchers had been excluded by being at Camp I. They claimed that David Peterson had gone round persuading the Sherpas against the South Col route; the Sherpas certainly realized that carrying loads up fixed ropes and sliding down again was less work than slogging through deep snow stamping out a new route to the Col. The Latins said John Evans had ordered the Sherpas to move all the Ridge equipment over to the Face pile after the decision had been made. Ned Kelly of the BBC, who was operating the radio at Base Camp, was accused of falsifying messages.

The atmosphere was one of bitterness and recrimination against the leaders, the Face team and the expedition at large. I was immeasurably sad to see my close friends of yesterday so grieved. I could sympathize with their feelings of frustration yet not agree with their expression of them. The predominant emotion was one of sadness that it had all ended up like this; their personal disappointments were not overtly discussed.

Later that day Norman Dyhrenfurth descended to Base Camp with Duane Blume, who had stayed up to see that his oxygen system was working satisfactorily. Norman was unwell, suffering from a very sore throat.

As they came into camp, Yvette Vaucher pelted Norman with snowballs. Later she hurled some stones at his tent and cut down the Swiss, French and Italian flags from the line that hung between the radio masts. Undue attention has been paid to these childish outbursts. Yvette was very distressed; she was a friendly and, up to that moment, a much-liked member of the expedition and it is only fair to make allowances for these insignificant but regrettable episodes.

At supper the atmosphere was tense. Jimmy Roberts was still down at Gorak Shep officiating at Harsh Bahuguna's cremation. He returned next morning having climbed Kalapatar, the hill above the yakherds' encampment, in order to have a good view of Everest and to see if there was any sign of movement on the Face. He watched some birds through his binoculars and ambled up to Base Camp oblivious of the furor that had blown up in his absence.

After a briefing from Norman Dyhrenfurth, Jimmy summoned Lhakpa, the assistant sirdar, to the kitchen and asked his opinion. He said Sona Girme had radioed from Camp II that the Sherpas were all in favour of the Face. Jimmy had urged this course since immediately after the accident. He confronted the Latin contingent and made a peremptory and final decision.

"No South Col; Face only, and if you don't like it you can go. There will be no discussion."

Jimmy's approach, however honest and direct, was not tactful and it infuriated the Latins, who decided to quit on the spot. They threatened to crucify the leaders at press conferences on their return to Europe and there were mutterings about letting off the oxygen bottles. As a hundred and fifty cylinders still remained at Base Camp, amounting to several thousand dollars' worth, a day and night guard of Sherpas was mounted against a wave of reprisal.

On the first day of May my patients were recovering from their various ailments and I was feeling much better. Michel Vaucher came into the hospital and I carefully examined his leg. The inflammation in the vein of his calf had subsided and I told him that he could have gone back up the mountain, but reaffirmed my view that the precaution of descending to Base Camp to recuperate had been wise. I had a deep affection for Michel, who was one of my best friends all through the expedition; we were linked by a common bond of speaking French and a mutual respect for each other in our widely different skills. I was sad to see him miserable, so unable to change a chain of circumstances that seemed to have been thrust on him and against which he felt powerless. Yvette came in.

"Are you still giving us medicines?" she asked sadly, crying. "I have a bad pain in my tooth."

"Of course," I said. "It makes no difference to my job, all this awful business." She softened and became her warm self again and cried onto Michel's shoulder. I gave her some pain relief for her toothache. Later Carlo came in and I had another sad talk with a very good friend. Circumstances seemed to have mastered his situation and himself too, as he had been swept into a vortex far beyond his power of control.

At dinner one could predict a confrontation, and it came; yet I feel sure it might have been avoided. Instead of amicably forgetting our differences for the last night and all sitting together, the leaders and the predominantly Anglo-American members sat down at one end of the mess tent while opposite and separated by a short distance were the Vauchers, Mazeaud and Mauri with Juréc Surdel, Odd Eliassen and myself.

John Evans arrived late having come down from the Hill and gave a first-hand account of events on the mountain. "Camp VI has been established and occupied this morning by Don and Dougal. The oxygen sets are working well and only minor troubles have been found with the rubber valves freezing up. Hopes are rising for the summit and morale is on the up."

Yvette got up from the table to go to bed and upbraided John Evans in an emotional tirade, sarcastically thanking him for letting them down over the vote. John took it with characteristic calm and charity but the fuse was ignited and the charge exploded soon after. As Michel Vaucher, Carlo Mauri and Pierre Mazeaud left the tent, the latter threw some provocative taunts at Norman and the encounter began in earnest. The Latins were down one end of a long table, the leaders at the other end and various members ranged on both sides.

All the old arguments were produced, the old ground ploughed over, and the tent took on the air of a courtroom. Pierre Mazeaud, *magistrat, député, membre de l'Assemblée Nationale*, was in his element holding the floor with a powerful command of language and rhetoric. He cut a fine figure leaning on the large teapot, his index finger pointed and wagging. Carlo and Michel sat by and said little. I translated for them when they misunderstood the English.

Norman sat back at the end of the table and listened with attention and dignity as Mazeaud's loquacious accusations poured out: the Anglo-Saxon plot to oust the Latins, collusion with the BBC to put a Briton on the top for the success of their film, Whillans standing to make a million from his boxes if he reached the summit, allegations of drunkenness and pot smoking at Camp II, distorted radio messages over the vote. He rounded off with a personal thrust, "*Norman, tu est intelligent mais tu est faible pas comme ton père*" ("Norman, you are intelligent but you are weak, unlike yor father").

One man, a BBC cameraman, had been sitting quietly; his head was buried into his chest as he dozed off the effects of the whisky that had been circulating freely. In the middle of Mazeaud's most poignant plea for reconsideration of the decision on the South Col he stood up, lurched forwards and fell across the table, dislodging his spectacles.

"Look, another drunken Englishman!" shouted Mazeaud. "You are all drunkards and idiots."

Jimmy Roberts, who had remained notably silent in the face of the onslaught, leaned forwards and slowly, deliberately and with power of feeling, said, "Fuck off, Mazeaud."

Mazeaud's mouth drooped in horror. The bubble burst and a peal of hysterical laughter rent the air, doing nothing to placate the now furious Frenchman. Jimmy called for sirdar Lhakpa and, speaking in Nepali, told him to muster a squad of Sherpas outside the tent in case of trouble. But they were already there. Eager faces stood back in the shadows, hanging on every moment of the action.

Nothing much remained to say. I wrote home: "I am thin as a spindle, ten and a half stone (67 kilograms) and putting on weight but longing for steak, mushrooms and fresh tomatoes." It was so deliciously irrelevant.

The following morning, after a filmed interview, the Vauchers, Carlo Mauri and Pierre Mazeaud departed. I felt unhappy seeing them disappearing down the moraine and wondered why all this had come about.

I could sympathize with many of their sentiments. They were four people who had been built up by the publicity the expedition had engendered in their own countries to be the first Italian, the first Frenchman, the first woman to set foot on the top of Everest. Inseparable from this publicity was the possibility of certain prestige.

When the continentals' route on the mountain was no longer a reality, any chance they might have had of reaching the top disappeared; they were understandably disappointed but so were a lot of other people. I have no doubt in my own mind that abandoning the Ridge or Col route was correct, as indeed I had suggested immediately after the accident. That they were unable to arrive at an agreement and join the Face effort was sad. I think things might have turned out very differently had they not had so volatile a spokesman, or had the actual climbers themselves been able to decide the future of the climb on their own without others influencing their opinions. The dissension gathered momentum until the final outcome was inevitable.

The world press, being gluttons for scandal, seized this incident and splashed it across the headlines so that it was supposed to be the cardinal cause of the failure of the expedition. I must stress in the most powerful terms I can that this was a lamentable episode, in an expedition otherwise outstanding for its lack of tension and genuine comradeship. We had much cause to regret the press reports and could only be thankful that Murray Sayle's articles in the *Sunday Times* were giving a steady, honest and well-balanced coverage to the expedition.

But a number of well-known mountaineers were quoted in the papers, which arrived in the mail at Base Camp when we were just beginning to regain our spirits and confidence after the tragedy, and in the middle of all our political problems. This made us very angry and did nothing to ease our gloom — as if we had not enough to contend with already.

A magazine strung together, out of context, a lot of quotations from three climbers, Eric Shipton, Joe Brown and Ian McNaught Davis, which had a thoroughly demoralizing result.

"I was talking to a well-known climber who's been on several expeditions and he told me he'd actually pay *not* to go on this one."

"Nothing would persuade me to go on it ... do or die you bloody well do it. You have been paid to do it."

"... contains all the requisites for a great deal of ill feeling. I should think it would be absolute hell."

"... Mountains kill. One out of every ten climbers in the Himalayas gets chopped."

"On these big monstrous expeditions they can't afford failure but on the South-West Face they might easily fail. So they can always say afterwards 'We did the West Ridge and so were successful.'"

Even Lord Hunt and Sir Edmund Hillary launched into comment about our inevitable failure long before it happened.

We were sad that no one had any word of encouragement for us at a time when we most needed it. We felt like a man who is being kicked when he is down, and these comments came particularly ill from people many of us considered our friends.

But in the same mail as these miserable pieces of newsprint we received a copy of *Playboy* which had a different effect on us and did not remain intact for long. After passing quickly round the few expedition members remaining at Base Camp it fell into the hands of the Sherpas. Soon it was dismembered and the centre page was found decorating the tent of the sirdar and other pin-ups appeared in Sherpa tents all round the camp. The lack of interest in the magazine shown by the expedition members was interesting. When men are grouped together sex features high on their subjects for thought and discussion. But high altitude definitely has a depressant effect on their libido. When sex was mentioned on the mountain it was only in passing; none of the usual male obsession with the subject was evident. Men's animal priorities were ranged on very elemental planes: food and warmth took precedence over all and sensual appetites were relegated to a low place. Only when we were past Thyangboche on the way home did interest resurge with a vengeance as we began to notice for the first time what we had been missing during the past months.

Stuck at Base Camp, I settled down to live out the next weeks as best I could, hoping time would pass quickly. Every morning I woke and looked at my automatic watch, dreading that it might not have turned on to clock up one more day. By some brief mental arithmetic I worked out that I must be home in a month and I began to tick off the days in my head.

All the action was up on the Hill; the Latins had left and some of the sick people were down the valley recuperating. Few of us remained at

Base Camp and the place was lonely. I held clinics for the Icefall porters who were still making a daily ferry up to Camp I. By now the hazards had become a joke and they would come down laughing at how a large piece of the "mane wall" had broken off the previous night and how one of them had fallen into a crevasse. They were magnificent men, always cheerful and carrying out perhaps the most dreary, dangerous job in the world.

During much of the day I read at my desk in the hospital, I wrote letters home, listened to the BBC overseas news and occasionally took a tub bath. For my ablution I collected two pails of hot water from the kitchen and a deep tin pan; I rolled back the flooring of cut-down cardboard boxes, stripped down naked and poured hot water over myself with a mug. On a sunny day when the hospital had warmed up, a bath was refreshing and cleansing. I washed my hair with a lice-killing shampoo and changed my clothes. Compared with Camp II, where clothes were worn for weeks on end without washing, it was sheer luxury to be able to scrub them and dry them in the sun.

After lunch I sometimes slept to help the time pass and by evening the air was chilly and thick down suits had to be worn. I always went to the kitchen before supper to see Danu the cook, with whom I was good friends. We talked in Nepali and I heard many snippets about the expedition from the Sherpas gathered there that I would otherwise have missed. Danu gave me a mug of rakshi that had been brought up from Namche by his wife and I smoked a pipe and relaxed in the company of these men for whom I have a deep affection. Wood burnt in the fire and I could take off my boots to warm my feet on the hot stones that supported the cooking pots, and gaze at the dancing flames that echoed thoughts of more comfortable days.

We sang Nepali songs, many of which have beautiful words and tender meaning:

> Eh Kanchha, malai sun ko tara khasai deuna.
> Girl: O Darling, please pluck a golden star for me.

Tyo tara matrai hoina
Boy: Not only one golden star.

Jun pani khasai diu la.
I will pluck them all for you.

Gai goru bandhera
When you have tied up the cattle

chittai bhetnu aunu.
come quickly to meet me.

Batoma rat parla,
On the way the night will come,

ujyalo mai aunu.
so come when it is still light.

The Icefall Sherpas arrived back late in the afternoon when the snow flurries had started and they would have many stories to tell of the day's work. Supper was sometimes cheered by opening a bottle of whisky and soon after we would retire to bed to read by candlelight and think of home.

Chomolungma, the world's top dog, had grown now and was a large, yapping puppy. She had already made friends with a stray mongrel from down the valley that had found its way up to Base Camp, and together they howled in the moonlight. One night, having been kept awake twice before, I crawled out into the cold night air and aimed some stones at the maddening animal. My throw was wildly inaccurate and missed Chomo, hitting Danu's tent by mistake and waking all the occupants, who thought they were being attacked. Loud shouts came from inside the tent and Chomo made a dash for the hospital and had the cheek to jump into my sleeping bag. Meanwhile the camp broke into an uproar much louder than the dogs had made and Jimmy's voice roared an order to be quiet.

So peace fell on the camp again; Pumori stood above us, the glacier creaked and heaved and the avalanches thundered down off the enclosing walls at intervals during the long night.

CHAPTER 15

Soon I had no time to be bored as illness hit the expedition yet again. Each morning I went to Lil Bahadur's tent to make the radio schedule with the upper camps as I had been asked by Jimmy Roberts to take charge of this. By means of radio contacts, mostly with David Peterson and Murray Sayle at Camp II, and first-hand news from men coming down off the Hill, we were kept fairly closely in touch with activities on the Face.

On May 3, Reizo Ito was sent down from the Face, in a state of exhaustion, by his comrade Naomi Uemura. Jon Teigland and David Isles appeared in Base Camp, sick. Leo Schlömmer also came down, having stubbed his thumb on some ice; he was disgruntled, complaining that he was given no chance to lead on the Face. His moans got no ear and he was summarily told by the leaders to go back up and get on with the job.

The next day we heard that Don Whillans, Dougal Haston and Naomi Uemura were at the foot of the 1,000-foot (300-metre) wall that stretches like a black barrier across the upper part of the Face. They were fixing ropes and looking for a site for Camp VI, which would be sheltered from the continual barrage of stones that bombards the only places level enough to pitch a tent on. They said they hoped to put Camp VII at the top of the wall. Our hopes rose and I wrote, "We badly need success now to compensate for all our set backs."

May 5 was my birthday but I forgot all about it until tea time. John Evans, Wolfgang Axt and Odd Eliassen went back up the Icefall, feeling better. Odd never really recovered after Harsh's death and I was expecting he might come back again soon. Ned Kelly and John Cleare went up to strengthen the BBC team, while Pin Howell and Gary Colliver set off down the valley to convalesce from pneumonia and taste the pleasures of grass and rhododendrons. They both had an area of collapsed lung that was consolidating in the healing process. Until it could re-expand they were breathing with half a lung only and at altitude the consequences of this, added to the devitalizing effect of the illness itself, were serious. To send them up the mountain again before their lungs were functioning normally would have been extremely foolish. I celebrated my birthday with a swig from the bottle of medicinal whisky that was kept in the hospital and turned into bed early.

On May 6 John Evans came down, having gone no farther than Camp I when sickness hit him; Odd Eliassen was also ill and unable to go on into the Cwm. John Evans complained of a very sore throat and cough as well as feeling unusually weak. He was an immensely strong man and so dedicated to going back up to Camp II to help the men on the Face that I knew his symptoms must be genuine. I made a careful examination; his throat was red and inflamed but there was no pus on the tonsils; a tiny ulcer lay on one side of his throat and he had a mild conjunctival discharge from his eyes. His temperature was only a little raised and so far the signs did not add up to much. I examined his neck and there I felt a chain of small discrete glands in a line down both sides of the posterior triangle. This led me to look for more glands, which I found under his armpits and in his groin.

Suddenly a thought flashed through my mind: Norman Dyhrenfurth had come to me that same morning, having felt rotten in the night with a fever and a very sore throat that had become worse several days before and of which I had written in the medical record "virus-type illness." I had found a small ulcer on the underside of his tongue and he had a mild conjunctivitis but I had not noticed any glands. Could it be the same illness?

"Hang on, John," I said. "Make yourself comfortable and listen to a tape. I'll be back in a minute."

I went over to Norman Dyhrenfurth's tent, where he was lying in his sleeping bag feeling wretched and barely able to speak.

"Can I have another look at you, Norman? I think I may have found something."

Yes, the glands were present in all the expected places; I just had not noticed them before because in the cold I did not usually ask patients to undress fully for examination.

This must surely be glandular fever. I wrote home:

God knows how many more will succumb. What an ill-fated expedition this is. Norman says there has been more sickness on it than any previous party he's known, not to mention the weather and all our other problems. Now we have only four climbers capable of carrying on up the Face and they have been lashed by storms for the past three days and can only tolerate so much of that sort of treatment. I fear for Dougal's feet in these conditions. Today they are snowed up at Camp II. Time is running short.

I asked Duane Blume to find me a spare *Physician's Manual* that I knew David Peterson kept in his tin trunk. It was all there. Symptoms: fever, sore throat, glands, tiredness, aching. Complications: hepatitis, jaundice, ruptured spleen, meningitis.

I sent Ang Tsering to ask Jon Teigland and Odd Eliassen to come to the hospital. Their malaise and weakness over the past few days and the other symptoms all fitted the picture and on top of all the other signs I could feel the tip of Jon's spleen, which was an ominous sign. I sent a radio message by Lil Bahadur to Kathmandu asking for a schedule the next day with Dr. John Dickenson from Shanta Bhawan. The radio set was so powerful I was able to hear him clearly, as on a telephone, despite the distance and the intervening mountains. I told him the signs and symptoms of the illness and he confirmed my clinical diagnosis without reservation, which gave me much-needed reassurance for which I was truly grateful.

My predicament must be incomprehensible to doctors who are accustomed to working in an environment well-insulated by laboratories and x-rays and with colleagues always at hand to discuss their problems. Making a diagnosis of a condition with as many serious implications as this one in our particular situation was a frightening responsibility.

Four men now definitely had the illness and undoubtedly more would succumb. I thought that the infectious contacts must have been made several weeks before and so I saw no point in segregating patients.

I was especially worried over Norman Dyhrenfurth as I had weaned him off steroid treatment for his thyroid complaint early in the expedition and was afraid that this present illness, which he suffered much worse than the others, might cause a recurrence of the trouble and precipitate a thyroid crisis. So I started Prednisone treatment again and discussed with him the possibility of returning home.

"We're nearly through on the mountain, Norman, and it must all be settled one way or another in ten days. You're not going to get better up here and frankly there's not much you can do at this stage. If you do go out you might as well go all the way home to Europe and dampen the newspapers by telling the truth. What do you think?"

"I feel pretty awful, Peter; I agree with you I'd better go on down," Norman said sadly. As if he, our leader, had not had enough with his personal sickness and the depression that naturally accompanies virus diseases; this was a stunning blow and he could see all his labours over the past two years, all his plans for these months, crumbling around his ears with the knowledge that he faced a red-hot furnace of criticism and acrimonious debate on his return to Europe.

On May 8 the weather was bright and we heard better news on the radio. Camp V was established at 26,500 feet (8,100 metres) at the foot of the rock band, where two Whillans boxes and one tent had been put up and occupied by Don and Dougal. Naomi Uemura had come down, after helping pitch Camp V, to Advance Base Camp for a rest and Reizo Ito was staying in Camp IV.

Jimmy Roberts sent a message up the Hill to Don Whillans over the radio that morning, appointing him climbing leader and leaving all decisions about advance, choice of route and retreat to his discretion. Only four of them remained up there and now they must climb the mountain by any means they knew. All we could do below was to follow their progress with every radio contact and wish them luck.

Early that morning Duane Blume came to me coughing heavily after a sleepless night. He complained of an agonizing pain in his chest that was due to a small fracture of one of his ribs caused by an excessive bout of coughing. Having suffered similarly a month before I wasted no time in making a diagnosis. But he also had the tell-tale glands all over his body and the same symptoms as the others.

Duane felt very rough. "The oxygen's all working, Peter, there's nothing I can do to help it down here. What d'you think I should do?"

I gave him the reply I knew he wanted and suggested he accompany Norman down to get the plane at Lukla. He was booked to leave early anyway, so a day or two made little difference.

As he hobbled sadly out of Base Camp, looking a lot older since his experiences of the past few weeks and no doubt a lot wiser, I marvelled at the transformation that had come about in him. He joined us a folksy Midwesterner wildly contrasting with his athletic companions. He organized all the oxygen equipment and put on crampons for the first time in earnest to climb up the Icefall. For four weeks he had taken over the radio communication at Advance Base Camp, keeping up people's spirits under the awful conditions in the blizzard, and he made impassioned pleas for sanity during the crisis with the continentals. Duane had worked as hard for this expedition as any man, with utter loyalty and integrity, and had emerged as a person with sound judgment and strong character of whom small-town Bishop, California, had good reason to be proud. But now

I saw him bowed out by illness and felt sorry to see my chess companion go down.

Norman followed Duane and all the Sherpas came out to shake his hand and wish him well. He could barely croak his thanks to them and their sadness was evident as their leader left the camp that had cost him so dear to build. If only for his sake, we needed success desperately now. What is the driving force that pushes him to undertake such an endeavour? It cannot be fame, for 1963 brought him personally very little, even though he shook the hand of President John Kennedy in the White House rose garden. Certainly it is not money as he took nearly three years to pay off his debts on that occasion.

Perhaps he is trying to emulate his illustrious father — an expert in Himalayan geology and geography who led an international expedition to Kanchenjunga in 1930. The organization itself almost seems the *raison d'être* of his labours. He spent a large amount of his time worrying about business and finance, unable to throw himself completely into the expedition and enjoy it as he deserved. But knowing how much was at stake in terms of hundreds of thousands of dollars, his anxiety was understandable.

Norman was sick with a rare inflammation of the thyroid gland before leaving Europe; this possibly caused him to be more anxious and tense than usual. Perhaps he was just older, having just turned fifty, but he had moments of deep depression and despair on the expedition. He would slump in a heap in the mess tent, moan about the money that was yet to be found, and he was in need of much reassurance and encouragement.

No one could doubt Norman's idealism. He really believed in the concept of an international adventure and was determined to make it work. Many would question the way he set about it, his choice of personnel, his claim that the "true" West Ridge was a really new route on Everest; but his sincerity was beyond reproach.

Just before Norman departed, Lhakpa talked to Sona Girme at Camp II in a staccato, disjointed mixture of Sherpa and English, ending every passage with "Roger, Roger, Over," followed by a throaty chuckle.

They shouted at each other, thinking that volume would speed their messages up and down the Icefall. Through the static and the aberrations of our receiver, which needed frequent thumps from Lil Bahadur's powerful fist to jolt it into action, we understood from Sona Girme, "Camp II is hopeful. We're sure they'll make it." So Norman left with a ray of encouragement, followed by John Evans, Odd Eliassen and Jon Teigland, who were descending to Kunde for convalescence.

David Peterson spoke to me on the radio that evening. Reception was very poor but I understood that Antony Thomas, the BBC film producer, was coming down suffering from frostbite. Dave was at Camp II and had become the Camp II manager overseeing the movement of supplies up onto the Face and was doing a fine job. He was sticking closely to our agreed policy of sending down to Base Camp any members who were sick, after starting first aid treatment. Juréc Surdel, the Polish West Ridge cameraman, was also coming down ill.

May 9 was a busy day, and now that I was so fully employed the days were flying by and I had difficulty in believing the date dial of my watch that was ticking over with such speed.

I prepared the hospital to receive Antony Thomas, not knowing how bad his frostbite would be. Danu was heating plenty of water on the fire in the kitchen and had bowls ready for bathing. Antony came in late in the evening with a note from Dave Peterson. The BBC man was walking on his own and wearing his loose-fitting camp boots. I put him to bed in the corner in Ang Tsering's place, the latter having moved into a nearby tent.

Antony had been working hard filming at Camp II and for the past week had not felt his toes, a common experience up there where one went for days on end with cold feet unless taking the precaution to warm them with a hot water bottle. He had not looked at his feet for several days. When he removed his socks he noticed some blisters and dark patches on the right big toe and some blisters on his fingers, which he brought to Dave Peterson's attention.

He could not feel a sharp pin prick in any of his toes and the black patch on the big one was dry and clean. Antony had always suffered from chilblains and poor circulation, so had not paid particular attention to his feet, although eleven days earlier he had been warned to take extra care because he was losing the feeling in his toes. But he tended to neglect himself when he was deeply involved in his work.

This was our first case of frostbite — a condition for which I had taken great precautions to prepare.

Antony Thomas was a pleasant companion during his ten-day stay in the hospital. We talked at length about our lives till the candles had burnt right down to their bases; the candle-light gave a warm glow and we felt secure against the wind.

Antony is a bright young producer who has won several medals for his documentary films. When he arrived in Kathmandu, none of us imagined that the handsome, chain-smoking young man in high-collared, well-cut suits would put on crampons for the first time and make six journeys up the Icefall and seven trips between Camp I and II, often in appalling weather. Sometimes his forays seemed planned to prove that he was as tough as any of us, which he did conclusively, but more often they were made purely in meticulous pursuit of his work. He spent several years after university working as an actor and later as a producer in South Africa, where he drank tea with Dr. Verwoerd, and was condemned to death for political reasons.

He took a detached and objective view of climbing that was very refreshing and he was positively appalled by the waste of money and life that our expedition had involved. He set out from Britain with the brief to make the "greatest climbing film ever"; certainly it turned out to be the most expensive. Owing to illness of many of the film team, no professional stayed higher than Camp II so there were very few high camera shots; but he may certainly get an expedition film of unrivalled human interest. In our discussions we found much in common, especially our hatred for Everest and its Base Camp and our love for South Wales, where we both had mountain retreats. We were able to indulge our nostalgia unashamedly and thereby gained much moral support and comfort. I dressed his feet daily to keep them clean and watched them slowly recover.

Bill Kurban, a BBC soundman, was our second case of frostbite. He was once a marine commando and had shown that he was tough and determined since early on in the expedition, although he had no experience on mountains.

Ned Kelly of the BBC tried to radio down from Camp III at 1 p.m. one stormy day towards the end of the expedition but his voice was unintelligible. Bill Kurban said he must go up to see if Kelly was in trouble and to find out what was wrong with the set. He started off from Advance Base at 3 p.m. in approaching bad weather, with his Gurkha kukri knife strapped to the rucksack he carried on his back. He had already made the journey to Camp III on three previous occasions and knew there should be spare sleeping bags left there, so he was not carrying one. He promised John Evans, who was back directing operations on the Face, that he would return if he had not reached the bergschrund by 4:30 p.m. When he got near the fixed ropes he took off his rucksack, in which his duvet jacket and other warm clothing were packed, "in order to move faster." He climbed the fixed ropes, to which his jumars were clipped, and was wearing crampons on his boots.

About 7 p.m. the Sherpas from Camp III heard shouts which must have come from the foot of the Face, where John Evans and two Sherpas had followed to bring Kurban back to Camp II.

Lhakpa Nuru said to Ned Kelly, "Expedition sahib coming."

Kurban was two-thirds of the way up the fixed ropes on the steep snow slope below Camp III. As it was dark, two Sherpas went down with lights to help him and they brought him up to Ned Kelly's tent. He was wearing thick down gloves, a scarf and duvet trousers with only a pullover on his top. On arrival at Camp III it was dark but he carried out a simple maintenance problem on the faulty aerial. Kelly said Kurban was cold, tired and mumbling about some sugar that he produced, asking Kelly if he would like to try some of it.

They dressed Kurban in a duvet, put him into a single-thickness inner sleeping bag and gave him some hot soup. He settled for a while and then said, "I want a pee."

"Do it through the door flap, there's no need to go outside," said Kelly.

"No, I'm going outside," Kurban retorted adamantly.

"Be careful then and hold onto the ropes," warned Kelly. Kurban opened the zip and went out of the tent door, which overhung nearly a thousand feet (three hundred metres) of steep ice, and slipped while he was passing water. He was fortunately holding one of the fixed ropes that surrounded the tent and was brought to a sudden halt before he gathered momentum. Sherpa Lhakpa Nuru and Ned Kelly pulled him back into the tent. In spite of taking a sleeping tablet, he shouted throughout the night about the radio and sundry unrelated matters. Once he turned to Kelly and said, "Will you come with me to Kathmandu to get some fresh fruit?"

By 3 a.m. Kelly had not slept and Kurban announced, "I want to go down." During the hours before dawn broke he messed around trying to put his boots on. At 6:30 a.m. the first light crept into the tent but the sun never hit Camp III until ten o'clock and so it was still bitterly cold.

"I want to get going," Kurban told Kelly, who was nodding off to sleep for the first time that night. He went outside onto the small snow ledge on which the camp was pitched and started putting his crampons on without gloves, so the freezing metal was in contact with his unprotected fingers. After a while he gave this up and took his boots off.

Ned Kelly talked to David Peterson now that the radio was repaired and was advised to take no risk with anyone's life in getting Kurban, who was now becoming belligerent, off the mountain. At the top of the fixed ropes Kurban refused assistance from the Sherpas, clipped himself into his jumar and set off down alone, wearing his gloves.

Kelly radioed to David Peterson, telling him that a rescue party should go out from Camp II to meet Kurban. John Evans made record time to the bergschrund and found him well down the fixed ropes. Kurban was rubber-legged and falling every few steps. When he was 800 feet (240 metres) above John he skidded 200 feet (60 metres) down and caught himself on the fixed rope with his left hand only.

John said, "Gee, man, I didn't think you were ever going to stop." Kurban's harness was unbuckled and he was not secured to the ropes.

On the way down he suffered from hallucinations and claimed that he could see men lying in the bergschrund. He fell twice on the easier ground below and was held on the rope. Sona Girme came out to meet the returning party and Dave Peterson gave Kurban an injection of dexedrine before rapidly rewarming his fingers.

The only other person to have frostbite was Wolfgang Axt, whose feet had become very cold while waiting for Harsh on the day of the accident and never warmed up properly again while he was in the high camps. He was only slightly affected, with loss of sensation in his left big toe, the nail of which went black and looked as if it would fall off.

The weather conditions on the mountain being as bad as they were during the expedition, we were fortunate not to have more trouble with frostbite. As can be seen from the three cases we encountered, the degrees of severity of frostbite vary but the basic cause is the same — freezing of the tissues.

On a mountain all the circumstances obtain for severe chilling of the body. Low temperatures occur with increasing altitude and the wind blows with force for much of the time, giving extreme conditions of cold. The combination of low temperature and wind is the only true indication of the degree of cold and is known as the wind-chill index. If the sun is shining men can walk around in shirt sleeves in temperatures of −40°C provided no wind is blowing. In blizzard conditions with gale-force winds the thermometer need not be very low for extreme chilling to occur. Usually on high mountains the air is cold and dry, but should the person himself become wet owing to heavy perspiration or clothing becoming sodden with snow, this increases the degree of chilling.

In severe cold the body reacts to try to maintain the temperature of its core and all the physiological changes that take place are directed towards this end, since depression of core temperature may lead to death.

The blood vessels in the periphery constrict to keep the blood away from the skin where heat is lost to the exterior. Sympathetic nerves from the temperature-regulating centre in the brain cause the muscular coats of some of the small vessels, the arterioles, to contract and shunt the arterial blood directly into the veins, thus bypassing the capillary circulation to the skin and other tissues. Capillaries are tiny vessels with walls only one cell thick across which oxygen passes out of the blood to the cells of the body and carbon dioxide, the end product of cell metabolism, passes into the blood to be carried to the lungs and exhaled. The flow of blood in the periphery slows up due to the cold and this may be accentuated by the increase in stickiness due to acclimatization; as a result the peripheral tissues are deprived of oxygen and are more susceptible to damage. Clotting or thrombosis may also occur in the smallest vessels.

The capillary walls are damaged by freezing and the water constituent of blood, the plasma, seeps out into surrounding tissues, causing swelling and blister formation. Water is sucked out of the cells by ice crystals which form between them, causing dehydration of the cell and disturbing the delicate enzyme systems upon which normal function depends. Finally the water inside the cell itself may freeze. The nucleus will be destroyed and the cell will die. When a large number of cells are killed in this way gangrene results and the tissues turn purple, then black. In time the dead areas will separate from the living by a clear line of demarcation and "autoamputation" will result.

In exposure, the temperature of the body's core is severely lowered, all the vital systems slow down and eventually the heart stops beating. Harsh Bahuguna's death was ultimately due to exposure, though he had suffered from frostbite of his extremities some time before he died.

Exposure occurs not uncommonly on the British hills to walkers who become very chilled, having been caught out in wet, wind and cold without adequate protective clothing. In Labrador I had vainly tried to revive two drunken Inuit who had fallen off their boat and spent a quarter of an hour in the icy water before being rescued; their deaths were primarily due to exposure.

Under normal conditions the body can adjust the balance between production and loss of heat. Heat is produced mainly by the body's metabolism of food, which is like an engine burning fuel; heat is increased by exercise and shivering, itself a form of muscular exercise. Heat is lost from the skin and the lungs to the outside air; heat loss is increased from the skin by sweating and from the lungs by heavy breathing.

When exposed to cold, the body diminishes its loss of heat by constricting the peripheral blood vessels in the skin, making the hairs stand on end to trap the air, and by exercise and shivering. Warm clothing increases the body's insulation.

Factors that alter the body's heat balance for the worse are poor food and clothing; fear, exhaustion and loss of sleep; illness and immobility; and alcohol and smoking.

GARY COLLIVER returned to Base Camp on May 9 after six days down at Thyangboche convalescing from his collapsed lung, which was caused by the severe attack of pneumonia he suffered at Camp II.

"I don't feel any different from when I left, Peter," he said. "If anything I'm more tired." Gary was not given to feeling sorry for himself unnecessarily. I listened to his chest and found the lung had completely re-expanded and the breathing sounds were clear. But I noticed enlarged glands under his armpits and in his groin, and he had a sore throat and a general feeling of malaise. The picture was the same as the other "glandular fever" victims. Gary had walked down to Gorak Shep with three American hippies two days before he went up to Camp II at the end of April. He remembered sharing a cup with them while drinking tea and I wondered if this could have been the original contact from which the epidemic started.

But of far more serious consequence was a symptom Gary mentioned only in passing. "While I was climbing a hill below Thyangboche I noticed some blurred vision looking into the distance, and when I shut one eye and then the other, I found small bright patches where I couldn't see anything."

Two weeks before this he had complained of hazy vision coinciding with a frontal sinus infection and I had then found nothing abnormal on examining the back of his eyes. Now his symptoms were more definite, though they seemed to have improved slightly, and were obviously causing him some worry. I dilated the pupils of his eyes with atropine drops so I could examine the back of his retina clearly. The ophthalmoscope I had in my diagnostic set was far from ideal for a detailed view of his fundus.

I took Gary into the darkness of the hospital and spent a long time examining the backs of his eyes. Small hemorrhages, where blood had leaked between the layers of the retina, were easily visible near the focal point, the macula. The optic disc, where the nerve fibres enter the back of the eyeball and spread out centrifugally, was swollen and the veins dilated and tortuous; this papilledema caused me great concern. I tested his urine and found no sugar, and his blood pressure was normal. A few benign conditions are known to cause such swelling and it has been recorded as a specific complication of altitude, but something nasty, especially a tumour occurring inside the head, is a more common cause and must always be excluded first.

I explained the problem at length to him.

"I know this is mystifying, Gary, and I particularly don't want to scare you. You've had the hell of a lot of sickness to put up with but I really think this eye problem must be investigated soon, and at a big centre where they can get to the bottom of it."

"My wife worked at California Medical Centre when we were in San Francisco, so I guess they'd see me," he replied.

"Okay, I'll write them a detailed report," I said. "You're not fit to go up the Hill again, so why don't you go down and get on the same plane as Norman and Duane?"

"I guess I'll do that, Peter. What a hell of a business."

Gary Colliver had rotten luck all through the expedition and despite being one of the crack young American climbers and usually supremely fit he suffered one illness after another: stomach upsets, sinusitis, bronchitis, pneumonia, "glandular fever" and now this. He worked unstintingly for the expedition, packing food at Base Camp, in the Icefall, trying to break through to Camp I in the blizzard, and now he was going to leave having barely laid a hand on the mountain of his dreams. He took his disappointment bravely.

He returned to San Francisco and was subjected to a battery of tests and examined by several doctors who were fascinated by his case. After some weeks I received a letter from the professor in charge of the unit. "The findings are consistent with a diagnosis of benign intracranial hypertension which is slowly resolving." I felt very happy that any serious cause had been excluded, and satisfaction that the diagnosis of this fairly rare disease, which I had written in my original report made at Base Camp and sent to San Francisco, had been confirmed.

CHAPTER 16

Despite the expedition's appallingly depleted manpower, the men on the Face were still forging ahead slowly in the face of changeable and often impossible weather.

On May 9 Leo Schlömmer and David Peterson carried loads up to Camp III accompanied by John Cleare, who was trying to get some much-needed film shots on the Face. At these altitudes climbing is hard work but wielding a camera, to the freezing metal of which fingers are liable to stick, is akin to slavery. John Cleare stayed up for three days and went out above Camp III to film Naomi Uemura, who had come up from Advance Base and was on his way towards the high camps to give support to Don Whillans and Dougal Haston at Camp V. John had gone up soon after a fairly serious chest infection; he knew the risk he was taking but was determined to do some high filming, very little having been achieved so far owing to illness. He had been coughing that night. While filming he "felt very rough" and passed out while still clipped onto the fixed rope, which prevented him plunging down the Face. John was helped back to

Camp III and put to bed in a Whillans box by Naomi Uemura, who continued on his way up to Camp V. This little Japanese man with the permanent quizzical smile had the remarkable ability of being able to run up and down the Face as if it was a child's slide.

On May 10 Leo Schlömmer and David Peterson carried on up to Camp IV, Peterson returning the same day to Camp III. During the night Leo heard a strange whining noise, like the blades of a helicopter, fast approaching his tent accompanied by regular thuds, so he covered his head and lay still, waiting for the object to pass. He deduced that the missile was an oxygen cylinder displaced from one of the camps directly above — a new element of danger had entered into Himalayan face-climbing and became an accepted hazard. Leo went to sleep with his crash helmet on, which was just as well because later that night a falling stone ripped a hole through the tent and landed beside his sleeping bag. The whine of falling oxygen bottles could be heard from Camp II. At least they were being well-used, and the few minor problems reported from the high camps were no detraction from the overall success of Duane Blume's system.

The next day (May 11) David Peterson returned to Camp II and was told by Sona Girme, "The monsoon has reached the Bay of Bengal. You have five days to climb the mountain." Dave reported to Base Camp that he thought they would take eight to ten days to reach the top and we were very disappointed as we had hoped they were nearer. Jimmy Roberts had for some time made the 13th a tentative summit date, but this had been put back by the weather to the 18th, which was Don's birthday, and we thought a push for the top on that day would appeal to his sense of fun.

By May 13 we heard that Don Whillans and Dougal Haston had found the site for Camp VI at the bottom of the black wall at a height of about 27,000 feet (8,200 metres). Dougal's voice was heard over a very crackling, spasmodic radio asking Camp II for more climbing equipment, fixed rope, snap links and oxygen. Snow fell on Base Camp at lunchtime, which was a sure sign that the weather up the mountain had changed for the worse.

John Evans felt well enough to return to Camp II to direct operations in support of the Face. Pin Howell had been continuously unwell and was evidently unfit to return up the Hill, so he volunteered to start off on foot with one Sherpa and twenty porters to escort some loads back to Kathmandu. He would pick up Odd Eliassen and Jon Teigland, who were recuperating from "glandular fever" down the valley, and take them along with him. Jimmy Roberts felt that men who were not actively needed were better employed in beginning the gradual dismantling of Base Camp and being evacuated early, as a bottleneck was likely with too few small aircraft available to fly the large number of expedition members out of Lukla. The monsoon was imminent and would put an end to all flying when it arrived.

On the evening of May 14 Pembatharkay, the climbing sirdar on the Face, arrived at Base Camp sick and upset at having to leave the mountain. He had distinguished himself on Annapurna the previous year carrying loads to the highest camps over very difficult steep ground and was admired by Don Whillans and Dougal Haston, for whom he had developed an intense loyalty.

He had a cough fracture in the middle of his right eighth rib, our fourth case of this uncommon condition. I injected a long-acting local anaesthetic into the nerve that ran along the cracked rib in order to block off the pain, which was causing him much distress on breathing. But his main complaint was of severe stomach pains, which had been building up over the last few days. He was unable to keep food down, and vomiting and retching all the time made him feel weak and miserable. The next day Kanchha from Namche, the other climbing sirdar and formerly attached to the Ridge team, came down with exactly the same condition. He too was off his food, feeling nauseated and very tender over the upper part of his stomach.

Both men appeared to have acute erosions of the stomach and I began treatment with milk drinks and alkali medicines to neutralize the acidity of the stomach juices. This illness is potentially dangerous and an early acute ulceration of the stomach or duodenum can go on to massive hemorrhage into the bowels, such as the sirdar Ang Dorji had suffered on the march-in. Sherpa Pa Temba Pangboche had symptoms of an acute ulcer about one week before Pembatharkay and Kanchha.

I spent a long time talking to them beside the fire in the kitchen and both men had much to say about the mountain. Pembatharkay was optimistic, talking in the present participle as all Sherpas do, in fast abrupt speech.

"Maybe missing Camp VI, going straight to the top. Don and Dougal very strong. Don he says to me 'Pembatharkay, four more blokes like you four's all we need to climb this bleeding mountain.' Nima he was on Annapurna. We both carrying to top camp." He looked sad and bitterly disappointed.

"And what happens if the monsoon comes?" I asked.

"They still going to the top," he replied.

"Would you come back again?" I asked.

"Never," said Pembatharkay, "Sherpas climb because Jimmy asking us. I been on ten expeditions. Never one hard as this one. Climbing Camp III to V very steep, steeper than Annapurna. We climbing to Camp V with no oxygen; no oxygen for sleeping, no good Sherpa food. Camps very crowded, four men in a Whillans box."

Pembatharkay cheered up quickly when his pain had worn off.

"I go back up tomorrow, doctor sa'b?"

"Sorry, Pembatharkay," I said. "The climb's nearly over and you might get sick again and that could be bad."

"I going home then. Making rakshi for Don and Dougal coming down. Now no more Everest."

Kanchha looked miserable and in pain. The poor food up the mountain and being formerly a heavy rakshi drinker must have contributed to his ulcer. At Camp II during the blizzard we had talked much. He was less hopeful about the prospects on the mountain.

"The sahibs lie in the tents drinking oxygen. They could have gone to the top four days ago if they had moved quickly. The Sherpas are very fed up; they're pleased John Evans is going back to take charge."

Kanchha's comments were a bit hard as the men on the Face had impossibly high winds to contend with even when it was clear. For the last two days the Face could not be seen. We heard over the radio Dougal's voice, "We've made no progress out of Camp V; more than two feet (0.6 metre) of new snow is plastering the Face. We're out of heating gas and have had nothing to drink and no hot food. There's no way of drying our boots and it's bloody cold up here."

On May 16 Leo Schlömmer and Wolfgang Axt came through from Camp II to Base in a day, narrowly missing a powder-snow avalanche that came hurtling off the Western Shoulder. They also reported that the "mane wall" had finally collapsed during the night, by a stroke of incredible luck, and this made the middle of the Icefall considerably safer. They were disgruntled although perfectly fit. Wolfgang told his story.

"I was at Camp II for thirteen days asking Dave Peterson, who had made himself the king, for a chance to go on the Face. Every day I was told all the camps were full and there was no place for me anywhere."

On his return up the mountain in company with John Cleare, Wolfgang had said that he had no interest in the Face and only intended to return in order to clear up Camp III West and bring down the tents and Harsh's personal equipment that was left up there. He had also refused Don and Dougal's request for help soon after his return to Camp II, saying that he had promised his wife he would not go on to the Face as it was too dangerous. Leo Schlömmer claimed, "Don and Dougal have been out in front for two weeks and have not allowed anyone else through into the front camps. They are blocking the advance and they must change the lead around between the various Face climbers." This was true, but the background to his dissatisfaction needs to be understood.

Leo had become very unpopular with the Face team early on because, they said, he was so lazy. Now that the hard work of breaking trail on the lower slopes was over they were not willing to let him into the front just before the summit. Also Leo had no partner to climb with and as the British and the Japanese were naturally paired he was out on his own.

The suggestions of one pair "hogging the lead" were open to criticism because Don Whillans and Dougal Haston had proved themselves the most experienced rope in the expedition and at this stage, with all our setbacks, we desperately needed success. I wrote home, "So what it comes to is that two British, two Japanese and a bunch of Sherpas are left to climb Everest alone."

Seven Sherpas arrived at Camp II that day with John Evans, who again took command of the organization which David Peterson had been managing for the best part of two weeks; but Dave had got up against sirdar Sona Girme and the Sherpas were unhappy with the situation.

Murray Sayle had taken over the radio schedules and was very quick to reply to our requests from Base. The air was alive with codes and secret messages preparing for a possible summit success and plans to scotch the press vultures hanging round the bars in Kathmandu waiting to scoop the story. Tension was building up in both camps and the atmosphere was exciting.

Murray sent down his daily reports to be passed on to London, where they were pieced together by his editors into a single report. Murray was becoming so excited by the whole progress of the expedition and the tense expectation that was being infused into all of us that the objective reporting that was his brief became more and more personal. In London they were busy cutting out "we" and substituting "they" or "the Expedition." Murray was proud of holding the altitude record for reporters and no one would doubt the acclaim he deserves for this feat, although he spent more of his time prone than upright.

I awoke on the morning of May 17 and felt glands all over my body. My heart sank. Juréc Surdel came into the hospital with similar signs. Neither of us felt particularly ill, though Juréc had been suffering for a few days from malaise which I had labelled "Hy." on my notes.

Radio reception was good and we heard that Don and Dougal had placed a tent for Camp VI and they were hoping to move up next day. They had been seen from Camp II high on the Face, dragging the tents behind them.

"We're both well," reported Dougal. "We need only one or two days for fixing ropes and pegs on the rock band to be ready for a summit dash. We've got eight bottles of oxygen here." Reizo Ito had rejoined them after his short rest at Advance Base Camp, and Sherpas Sona Gyao and Ang Phurbu did a high-speed butane-gas carry from II to V to give them the heat to thaw themselves out.

The expectancy and uncertainty at Base Camp was agonizing but very exciting. Life revolved around the radio. Few of us were in the camp now; Jimmy Roberts, Sharma the Nepalese liaison officer, Juréc Surdel, Antony Thomas and I. Chomo had been sent down in disgrace to sirdar Lhakpa's house in Khumjung.

Ang Tsering and I spent some time packing the remaining medical equipment in boxes ready to be taken to Kunde Hospital when everything was over. His wife and ten-month-old baby had come up to stay for a few days so he was very happy. My friendship with Ang Tsering had grown steadily throughout the expedition. We had a pleasant and easy working relationship and I found him always keen to learn and quick to apply himself. He was at present studying an anatomy and physiology book for nurses that I had borrowed in Kathmandu. He was a good companion and I never found our proximity irritating. He was thankful not to have gone up the Icefall, which he dreaded. We often talked late into the night in the hospital; he cooperated with my wish to speak Nepali and we moved from one language to another with ease.

David Peterson asked to speak to me on the radio. "I'm mentally and physically sick of this place. I'd like to come down for a day or two."

"I don't think a change at this stage is justified, Dave," I told him. "The climbing's nearly over and we can't leave the boys on the Hill unattended. It really isn't worth us changing over for a couple of days. I'm afraid you'll have to stay, but I'll ask Jimmy what he thinks."

I passed on Jimmy's answer which was unequivocally "No," and after a silence Dave replied, "Well, I suppose I'll have to stay."

The weather at Base Camp on May 18 turned for the worse and above the Icefall we could see the Cwm like a boiling cauldron with clouds churning in the wind, so we held out little hope for progress on the Face that day. A fine dusting of snow covered the tents, adding to the air of desolation that always hung over Base Camp. The lammergeier vultures circled slowly in long sinuous curves like Gerard Manley Hopkins' *Windhover*:

> *Of the rolling level underneath him steady air, and striding*
> *High there, how he rung upon the rein of a wimpling wing*
> *In his ecstasy! then off, off forth on swing,*
> *As a skate's heel sweeps smooth on a bow-bend.*

From the Face they said, "We got up to Camp VI at 27,200 feet (8,800 metres) yesterday and we expect to occupy it today. Two Sherpas carried loads without using oxygen themselves to 26,000 feet (7,900 metres). As one of them said, 'No sahibs on the Face, only Sherpas.'" The Sherpas' working capacity was unlimited and they won all our admiration. They have so little to gain personally from hard work on this dangerous mountain and their financial rewards are small by our standards, and yet without them we could not have begun to climb it.

An avalanche had wiped out one small tent at Camp IV; luckily it was empty.

Dougal Haston's wife, Annie, and David Peterson's girlfriend had walked in from Kathmandu; when they arrived at Gorak Shep they sent a letter to Jimmy Roberts, who asked them to stay down there until they received a message to say that the men were coming down as he didn't want their presence in camp to affect the decisions of those on the Hill. On the evening of May 17 I learnt that two of the women's trekking friends were sick and they were worried about them, so I collected a bag of medicines and set off in the late afternoon with the Sherpa who had brought up the note. I told Ang Tsering to come after me hotfoot should I be wanted back at Base.

I took a couple of hours to reach Gorak Shep and arrived in lightly falling snow as darkness was approaching. I had lost my way in Phantom

Alley, which had changed out of recognition since I returned from Kathmandu in April. Much snow had disappeared from the ground, leaving bare rocks, many of which were left perched precariously on stems of ice, like toadstools. The melting ice made crazy patterns on the ground but the pinnacles had more sheen where the snow had disappeared, leaving bare water ice. The streams were full with melting snow and thundered past, carving deep undercuts as they swept round the bases of the ice towers, and the organ-pipe icicles dripped, hung and broke off like spent stalactites. The only sign of the track was the occasional pile of yak ordure and I missed the usual river-crossing, where a log bridge had been built, by keeping on the east bank for too long. When we realized our mistake we had to ford the fast-flowing stream by rolling large boulders down from the bank above until enough of them made stepping stones by which we could jump from one to another across the stream.

On arrival at Gorak Shep I found one of the patients had a severe infection in both kidneys that had been coming on for several days, and the other had pneumonia. Two other trekkers with whom they had joined up had bronchitis and were coughing up nasty yellow phlegm. I gave them all medicines and advised them to return to a lower altitude soon.

Beside a wood fire in the yakherd's little stone hut I chatted late into the night with Annie Haston, telling her of the progress on the mountain and all the latest news of Dougal, of whom she had heard nothing for a month. In fact I had seen Dougal very little myself for six weeks as we had always been in different places. We had passed as I went up to Camp II and he was coming down for a rest to Base in the middle of April; again as I was descending to Base after the storm and he was going up to Camp II we met in the Icefall near the "mane wall," which was no place to hang around for a chat.

Annie looked fit and suntanned from the walk-in although much rain had fallen, in keeping with the abnormal weather throughout Nepal that spring. I was surprised that her lower eyelids were rather baggy, showing up particularly by the low light of the flickering fire, but I paid little further attention to this.

I slept with the Sherpa boys in the hut and early the following morning I climbed the hill directly above Gorak Shep to get a view of the Face of Everest, intending to catch up with the women, who were going up to Base Camp where they had been invited for lunch by Jimmy Roberts. I had taken little exercise during the previous fortnight and on such a beautiful clear morning it was a pleasure to stretch my legs and fill my lungs. I enjoyed being alone again and as I rose a magnificent view of Everest unfolded. From the top of the hill, called Kalapatar (18,500 feet, 5,600 metres), Eric Shipton and Edmund Hillary for the first time saw the Icefall leading into the Western Cwm of Everest and the huge black face of the mountain itself.

The air was crystal clear: one tiny cloud hovered near the summit, quite still. "For sure there could be no wind up there today and the boys must be having a good day to climb," I thought. I felt uncannily close to them. The atmosphere was so clear that the intervening distance was grossly foreshortened and I could see the whole of the upper part of the Face. Did I see two specks moving to the right above the high ice field, towards the foot of the black wall? Even if they were not Don and Dougal I felt like yelling, "Good luck boys, we're rooting for you!" And I hoped the goraks soaring high above would carry the wishes of all of us across to them and to Naomi, Reizo and the Sherpas who were supporting them.

From the top of Kalapatar a view in every direction enabled me to pick out all the mountain peaks of the Khumbu, and I looked over the Lho La into Tibet where the North Shoulder of Everest stood. This place is steeped in history and I had a strange feeling of communion with all the other men in the past who had pitted themselves against the highest mountain of the world, many of whom were buried near its base. Chomolungma always wins; men and women challenge and even climb her but they never conquer.

I ran down the hill as clouds were already forming up to the south and moving up towards us, and I caught up with the two women half an hour from Base Camp.

On the news that morning Naomi Uemura reported that Don was estimating five days to the top and that Camp VII above the wall was not required. The Japanese expressed polite disagreement with Don on both counts. Naomi didn't mention it himself but John Evans learnt later from Don that he had verbally torn into Naomi the night before when the latter arrived at Camp VI with a load.

At suppertime Annie Haston complained of a headache and a pain down the back of her neck so I gave her two aspirins and she went to bed in a vacant tent. At breakfast the following morning she said, "I slept very badly last night and now my head feels like a balloon. The pain is worst over the back of my head and down my neck and the light is terribly bright." Her face was more puffy than on the previous day and a bluish tinge surrounded her lips.

"I think you'd better come into the hospital and let me have a look at you, Annie," I said. Already I was suspecting that the drama of the Spaniard was going to be re-enacted all over again.

With a few puffs of oxygen her colour improved, so I left the mask on and put her into a sleeping bag on the bed in the corner. After a quarter of an hour of breathing oxygen she said the pain in her head had eased. I felt sure she was suffering from high-altitude edema. Her face was swollen, her wedding ring was tight on her normally thin finger and her sock elastic had formed an imprint on her ankles. Annie told me that she was expecting her period, but this degree of swelling was more than she would expect with premenstrual edema.

I examined her carefully. Her temperature was normal, pulse rate a little raised to 100 and her blood pressure was 85/65, which was lower than the normal reading of 120/80. I could find no signs of fluid in her chest and her heart sounded normal. She weighed 113 pounds in her pyjamas on the hospital scales. Being a trained hospital nurse, Annie might have found her illness more frightening than an uninformed person, as she understood much of what was going on; but she was very philosophical.

"I think you've got a touch of the mountain sickness, Annie, but I'm sure I can manage you here till Dougal comes down. We should know one way or the other what is happening on the mountain tomorrow."

After a few minutes without the oxygen mask her headache returned, so I fitted her with the sleeping mask and gave her an injection of forty milligrams of frusemide, a diuretic drug to help her get rid of the water she was retaining, with instructions to measure all the urine she passed. She slept most of the day, only disturbed by having to pass water at frequent intervals. By the next morning she had passed 3,050 millilitres of urine in the previous twenty-four hours and her weight had dropped to ninety-eight pounds. Her face was less puffed and all the other swelling had subsided. This was proof that she had been retaining water in her body, described as an antidiuresis, which is the preliminary stage of acute mountain sickness and without treatment might go on to pulmonary or cerebral edema. I heard from Selwyn Lang, the doctor at Kunde, that a few weeks before a South Korean climber on an expedition to Lhotse Shar had been carried down unconscious from high-altitude cerebral edema, which causes the brain to swell. The patient was still not fully rational six weeks later after intensive treatment in hospital in Kathmandu.

I had reason to be very concerned over Annie Haston as people can die rapidly with this illness. I spent an anxious night watching over her and was relieved that she responded to the treatment. With the sleeping oxygen mask on her face she kept a good colour and regular breathing, but the mask kept falling off when she went to sleep and she turned a dusky colour again.

On the morning of May 21 we had a message from Dougal passed on from Camp II. "The climb's over, we're coming down." That was all. We felt sad but strangely relieved.

I wrote to Sarah:

With great sadness this morning we heard that Don and Dougal were abandoning their attempt on the Face. They have now spent more than twenty days above 25,000 feet [7,600 metres] and the final wall was just too much.

They said they were worn out and supplies of food, fuel, oxygen and rope were short. They would need another Camp (VII) and the climb would take another ten days at least. They have not the strength for that and the monsoon is approaching. The Japanese have earned all our admiration. They have supported the British pair unfailingly though their own chances of a summit were negligible. Naomi made two carries of oxygen bottles to Camp VI yesterday without using oxygen himself. Ito has been in support from Camp V. What an example of complete unselfishness in the cause of the expedition. What a fantastic pair of almond-eyed laughing little men! But surely you can't call it failure when the only four men left on the mountain can sit it out in terrible conditions on that huge, steep face and have it snatched from them so near success. I am proud to have been associated with them.

I asked Murray Sayle in confidence over the radio to pass on the news of Annie Haston to Dougal when he came down but not to alarm him. She was definitely improved in the morning but as she needed oxygen continuously I kept her at rest in the hospital.

Dougal and Don came down from Camp VI to Camp II by sliding down the fixed ropes most of the way. Don had a bottle of malt whisky stuffed inside his blue down suit from which he took swigs at every halt, so that by the time he was down he was in good form. He, Naomi and Reizo stayed at Camp II that night. Dougal came straight through after a brief rest at Camp II, past Camp I and down the Icefall alone. I went out to meet him at the foot of the Icefall at 5 p.m. as it was getting dark. Having descended nearly 10,000 feet (3,000 metres) in ten hours he was fairly done in and looked thin and haggard but surprisingly fit after the long siege of the past three weeks.

After Dougal had had a good strip wash in a hot tub in the hospital and the chance to be alone with Annie he came into the kitchen and told Jimmy and me what had gone on.

"Don and I realized when we left Camp II that we would have to stay in front until it was finished one way or the other. The Japs gave us great support, especially Ito, but they seemed a bit lost while leading. They kept talking about lack of campsites but there were quite a few around; I think they just lacked the Whillans cunning ...

"I have nothing but praise for Ito's effort. From the day he reached Camp V he worked as a Sherpa with never a word of complaint. Three more of his kind and there would be different headlines in the papers. Leo wanted a Sherpa to carry his own gear. The day we carried Camp VI Don and I used oxygen, but carried a load of rope as well as our personal gear. Naomi and two Sherpas made it without oxygen carrying a 'box' and cylinders ... altruism as opposed to self-interest. Camp VI was quite a place, almost impossible to stay warm unless one had a stove burning all night ... The wall above Camp VI was hard rock climbing at 27,500 feet (8,400 metres), harder work than anything we had to do on Annapurna and with oxygen on our backs and still a longish way to go to the top. When we finally quit we had no ropes, virtually no oxygen and food and only a dribble coming up. No way up, so you have to go down."

Naomi came down later that night with David Peterson and we sent a party out with lamps to guide them through the darkness. Naomi was full of praise for the Britons.

The following morning Annie Haston was a little improved but I wanted her moved down to a lower altitude as soon as possible, so I discussed the situation with Jimmy Roberts. She had to be escorted with oxygen, as I did not want to risk her falling sick on the way down; someone with a similar illness had recently died at Pangboche two days after descending from Kalapatar.

David Peterson was in Base Camp and could see the last few men safely off the Hill so I escorted Annie and Dougal down the valley, with Ang Phu carrying the oxygen set. She made a speedy and complete recovery on reaching a lower altitude.

Don Whillans came down that evening. He described bringing Murray Sayle through the Icefall as "the most frightening bloody time of my life. I just stood at bottom of each pitch with me arms open ready to catch 'im."

He told his story of the last few days.

"It was fantastically cold. We 'ad these 'uge mitts with fur but your fingers went wooden. It was 35 degrees below freezing and got hell of a lot colder. Even a light wind went right through you. We slept and climbed using oxygen but when the weather was bad we conserved it and just sat there feeling bloody miserable.

"When fixing ropes up a steep groove on the final 800-foot (240-metre) buttress the cold was intense. I rounded a corner and looked across the broken slabs of the Southeast Face and the original South Col route beyond them and tantalizingly close.

"I found the easy way up and I said, 'Right, we're not going that way to connect with the South Col. We'll go back and we'll have a crack at the gully.'

"I was just thinking about having a cigarette and looked up at the gully and thought, 'This is about three times as long as you thought it was, you're not going to get up this mountain, lad, and you're not going to come to no harm neither. Too crafty for that.'

"When Dougal came up I asked him, 'What do you think of it?' He said, 'Well, it's no' very difficult but it's a hell of a sight longer than I thought it was. We're going to need a lot more rope.'

Don looked at Dougal and could tell what he was thinking. "Well 'ow about buggering off?" he said.

And so we did.

AUTHOR'S NOTE

I WISH TO THANK Norman Dyhrenfurth and Jimmy Roberts for the chance of going to Everest and writing this book, which is a medical and personal account of the International Himalayan Expedition 1971.

So as not to transgress medical ethics, I asked permission from each member to write about the illnesses of the expedition. I am grateful to them for cooperating.

For all his hard work, and for his persistence in convincing me of the value of publishing this new edition of the book, most sincere thanks to my editor, Scott Steedman of Raincoast Books. Thanks also to my agent, Kathryn Mulders.

GLOSSARY

arak a strong spirituous liquor

bergschrund a large crevasse at the foot of a glacier head wall

Brahmin (also spelled **Brahman**) a member of the largest Hindu caste, with superior status; Brahmins are traditionally eligible for the priesthood

chhang a home-brewed barley beer

Chomolungma the Tibetan name for Everest, literally "Goddess-mother of the world"

chorten the Tibetan word for a Buddhist shrine; also called a *stupa*, from the Sanskrit

col a high mountain pass

coolie a porter or other unskilled labourer; from the Hindi word *Kuli*, a tribe from Gujarat, India

cwm an enclosed mountain valley

dokan a wayside teahouse where travellers can get a drink, a meal and a piece of floor space to sleep on

gompa a monastery

gorak a Himalayan crow

Gorak Shep name of a shepherds' encampment on the path up to Everest

Gurung a tribe of Nepali mountain people

Icefall, the an ice formation on Everest where the Khumbu Glacier spills out of the Western Cwm

kukri a distinctive Gurkha knife

Lho La a pass into Tibet over the western shoulder of Everest

momo Tibetan dumplings

Nangpa La another pass into Tibet

rakshi another strong spirituous liquor

sahib a term of respect often applied to Westerners; from the Urdu word meaning "friend" or "lord"

Sagarmatha the Nepalese name for Everest, literally "Goddess of the sky"

serac an ice tower in an icefall

Sherpa a tribe originally from Tibet that now lives in the Solu Khumbu district of Nepal; sometimes used to describe any high-altitude porter

sirdar a leader

Tamang a tribe of Nepali mountain people

Tashi Delek a Tibetan or Sherpa greeting

INDEX

ABOUT THE AUTHOR

A MEDICAL DOCTOR AND MOUNTAINEER, Peter Steele was born in England and has lived in Whitehorse in the Yukon since 1975. He ran the Grenfell flying doctor service in Labrador, travelling the coast by snowshoe, dog sled and boat. His first book, *Two and Two Halves to Bhutan*, told the story of his young family's adventures in that isolated Himalayan kingdom. He was the senior medical officer to the ill-fated International Himalayan Expedition 1971, an experience recorded in *Doctor On Everest*. He followed this with two books on medical care for climbers and *Atlin's Gold*, a slice of little-known British Columbian history. *Eric Shipton: Everest and Beyond*, a biography of the great English climber, won the Boardman Tasker Prize for Mountain Literature, and his next book, *The Man Who Mapped the Arctic: The Intrepid Life of George Back, Franklin's Lieutenant*, was a national bestseller shortlisted for a British Columbia Book Prize and a Banff Mountain Book Festival Award.